MODERN BOEING JETLINERS

Guy Norris and Mark Wagner

MBI Publishing Company

First published in 1999 by MBI Publishing Company, 729 Prospect Avenue, PO Box 1, Osceola, WI 54020-0001 USA

MBI Publishing Company books are also available at discounts in bulk quantity for industrial or sales-promotional use. For details write to Special Sales Manager at Motorbooks International Wholesalers & Distributors, 729 Prospect Avenue, PO Box 1, Osceola, WI 54020-0001 USA.

Library of Congress Cataloging-in-Publication Data
    Modern Boeing jetliners/Guy Norris & Mark Wagner.
        p. cm.
    Includes index.
    ISBN 0-7603-0717-2 (hardback: alk. paper)
    1. Jet transports. 2. Boeing airplanes. I. Wagner, Mark. II. Title.
TL686.B65N6824   1999
629.133'349—dc21   99-29418

On the front cover: Boeing's "Experimental Flight Test" logo on the side and the trailing static test cone hanging from the tail mark this otherwise anonymous- looking aircraft as the prototype 737-800.

On the frontispiece: A 737-800 bound for China Airlines of Taiwan is prepared for delivery in September 1998. A total of 65 -800s were delivered in that year

On the title page: A Cathay Pacific 747-400 nears the end of its journey at Hong Kong. Note the large satellite communications antenna located on the top of the fuselage aft of the hump.

On back cover, top: The 757-300 flight test program began on August 2, 1998, with a virtually flawless maiden flight. The only hiccup was the loss of the static trailing cone somewhere over the Olympic Peninsula, west of the Puget Sound area

On the back cover, bottom: The 767-400 fight deck layout was based on the large-format, 8-by-8-inch liquid crystal displays developed for the 777 as pictured here. The new layout added 21 new parts but removed 70 and provided flexibility to adapt to future air traffic control developments. Like the philosophy adopted with the Next Generation 737 flight deck, the displays could be programmed to show 747/777 style displays or the EFIS format of the existing 757 and 767 cockpits.

Edited by Mike Haenggi

Designed by Bruce Leckie

Printed in Hong Kong

CONTENTS

INTRODUCTION 6

ACKOWLEGMENTS 7

Chapter 1 BUILDING A FAMILY 9

Chapter 2 717: BACK TO THE FUTURE 25

Chapter 3 737: NEXT GENERATIONS 43

Chapter 4 747: ADVANCING THE LEGEND 73

Chapter 5 757: NEW DIRECTIONS 95

Chapter 6 767: STRETCHING AND GROWING 115

Chapter 7 777: THE MAGNIFICENT SEVENTH 125

Chapter 8 CREATING THE FUTURE 159

INDEX 175

INTRODUCTION

Boeing marches into the 21st century as the oldest, largest, and most successful aerospace company in the world. It has not been easy getting there, and Boeing knows it will need every lesson from the past to stay ahead of the competition and meet the challenges of 2000 and beyond.

Boeing grew dramatically in the 1990s with the purchase of Rockwell's aerospace business and the takeover of McDonnell Douglas. Although the integration of these massive organizations into the Boeing structure was far from painless, it was designed to produce a stronger and more vibrant company with sales close to $60 billion by the turn of the century.

As a result of these tremendous changes, the new Boeing is substantially different from the old. It now has far larger interests in military fighters, transports, helicopters, and missiles, as well as space vehicles, launchers, and information systems. Boeing's new-found diversity makes it far more flexible to meet the changing needs of the various markets it serves. The sheer breadth of product lines also makes it less vulnerable to the predictable waves and troughs that inevitably sweep through both the civil and military aerospace sectors.

Against this background, the jetliner family continues to be the backbone for the company. Of $56.2 billion in sales in 1998, around $35.5 billion was turnover generated by sales of Boeing jetliners. Even with reduced profits expected as a result of earlier production and development problems, the jetliner family was due to generate $66 billion in sales over the last two years of the century. The civil jet family is still, therefore, key to the company's continued prosperity and the focus for much of its investment.

To keep its jetliners competitive, Boeing has produced a string of derivatives that build on the best attributes of the past and combine them with the latest technological advances. The best example is the Next Generation 737, which became the fastest selling jet in history with more than 1,100 orders by the beginning of 1999. The strategy is tried and tested, having already twice extended the 737 line over past generations. Thanks to this policy, 737 orders, for all models, reached a staggering 4,234 by the end of 1998.

Deliveries of the new 737 family, the first 717s and 757-300s, were the highlights of 1999, another record year in which Boeing was expected to deliver an amazing 620 jetliners. In 2000, the new 767-400ER was due to take center stage with yet another 737 version, the -900, not far behind. Sales also continued to pour in with the backlog standing at more than 1,800 by early 1999. Together with sales of its recently acquired Douglas Aircraft products, the total Boeing order book climbed toward a phenomenal 14,500 later that same year. To ensure the first few years of the 21st century see these sales trends continue, the company is keeping a tight focus on its family of modern Boeing jetliners.

ACKNOWLEDGMENTS

A huge thank you to the many Boeing employees, past and present, who gave their time to inspire and assist in the creation of this book. They include Alan Mulally, Jack Gucker, Mike Bair, Borge Boeskov, John Hayhurst, Jeff Peace, John Roundhill, Jim Phillips, and Ron Woodard. We would also like to thank Jerry Callaghan, Tom Croslin, Tim Crows, Mike Delaney, Art Fanning, Ken Graeb, Dan Mooney, Joe Ozimek, Pete Rumsey, and Rolf Selge. For oiling the wheels of the project, we would particularly like to recognize Cheryl Addams, Ken DeJarlais, John Dern, Sean Griffin, Fred Kelley, Warren Lamb, Mike Lombardi, Tom Lubbesmeyer, Mark Hooper, Stephanie Mudgett, Debbie Nomaguchi, Robin Rees, John Thom, Ed Turner, and Fernando Vivanco. From the engine makers we also say thank you to Mark Sullivan and Robert Leduc of Pratt & Whitney; Norma Butters, Rick Kennedy, Pat Klaus, Jim Stump, and Jamie Jewell of General Electric; Gerard Laviec of CFM International; Barry Eccleston and Martin Johnson both formerly of IAE; Sara Sizer of Rolls-Royce; Caroline Harris formerly of BMW Rolls-Royce; and BNA's A. Scheel. The assistance of Helene Bloch, Robert George, Richard Hansen, and Tom Kilbane of Rockwell Collins Flight Dynamics is also greatly appreciated. Thanks also to the staff of Flight International, including Carol Reed, Graham Warwick, Gareth Burgess, Paul Lewis, Max Kingsley-Jones, and Andy "Hammers" Chuter. We are also grateful to John Bailey, Boutros Boutros, Stephanie Day, Robert Frelow, Captain Ian Johnson, Alison Lau, Captain Mike Livesey, Wai Lun, Andy Marsh, Tony Pereira, Erich Wagner, Sergey Sergeyev, Captain Ali Wells, and Knut and Sue Wilthil. For help, hospitality, and understanding, thanks to Leo, Sandi, and Megan Mitchell, Judy, Tom, and Greg Norris. As always, a big thank you to our editor, Michael Haenggi.

—*Guy Norris and Mark Wagner*

CHAPTER ONE

BUILDING A FAMILY

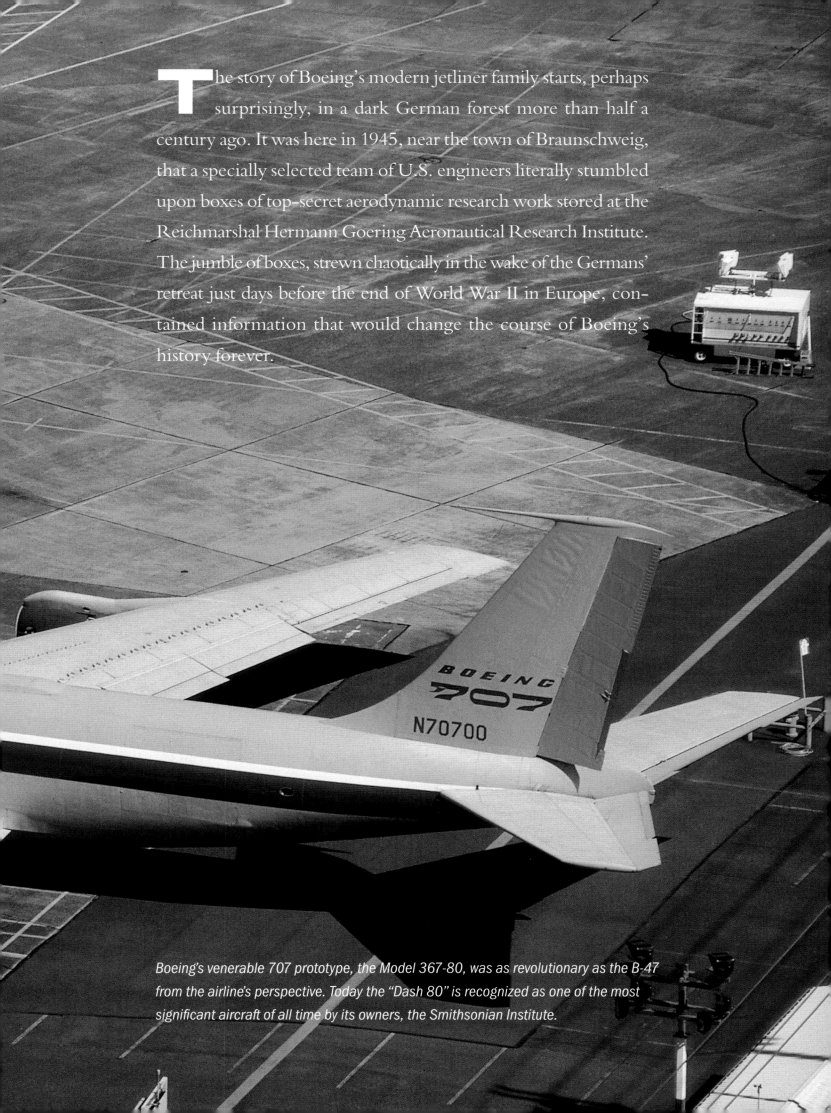

The story of Boeing's modern jetliner family starts, perhaps surprisingly, in a dark German forest more than half a century ago. It was here in 1945, near the town of Braunschweig, that a specially selected team of U.S. engineers literally stumbled upon boxes of top-secret aerodynamic research work stored at the Reichmarshal Hermann Goering Aeronautical Research Institute. The jumble of boxes, strewn chaotically in the wake of the Germans' retreat just days before the end of World War II in Europe, contained information that would change the course of Boeing's history forever.

Boeing's venerable 707 prototype, the Model 367-80, was as revolutionary as the B-47 from the airline's perspective. Today the "Dash 80" is recognized as one of the most significant aircraft of all time by its owners, the Smithsonian Institute.

The podded jets and swept wings of the B-47 established the blueprint for every successive generation of Boeing jetliner. Here an aging survivor displays its legendary lines at a museum in Pueblo, Colorado.

The vital data was wind tunnel research on swept-wing designs for jet-powered aircraft. Perhaps even more vital for Boeing was that three of the company's brightest engineers were on hand to witness the find and, realizing its significance, were able to send details straight back to their base in Seattle. The data arrived in time to profoundly alter the shape of a proposed new design—a jet-powered medium bomber and reconnaissance aircraft termed the XB-47.

Boeing's Model 450, complete with wings newly swept at 30 degrees measured at the quarter chord point, was declared the winner of the Air Force competition in October 1945. The radical wing sweep and podded jets caused a sensation when it was rolled out for the first time just under two years later.

The B-47 went on to form the phalanx of the U.S. Air Force's Cold War force and, at the same time, revolutionized the design

of all large and small jet-powered aircraft the world over.

Even Boeing underestimated the full significance of the B-47 on its own future. It was not until five years later, in 1952, that the first real commercial fruits of the design leap began to take shape. Ironically, the process again began with the military and the B-47. The Air Force's lumbering, piston-powered Boeing KC-97 tankers could not fly fast enough to refuel the new jet bombers without going into a shallow dive. The Air Force therefore issued outline specifications for a jet tanker/transport that could keep pace with the B-47.

Boeing responded with a company-funded $16 million gamble that was to give birth to the Boeing jetliner dynasty. The jet transport, dubbed the Model 367-80, was aimed at both the Air Force requirement and a new jetliner. The latter was to form Boeing's response to new jetliner designs emerging overseas, particularly the revolutionary British-built deHavilland DH-106 Comet that had caught the world off guard when it was first flown in 1949. The basis for the Boeing design had originated from the old Model 367 Stratoliner, but being the 80th rendition, had altered out of all recognition by the time the project was finally authorized.

The "Dash 80," as it was called, was rolled out of the Renton factory on May 14, 1954, and created as much of a stir as the B-47 had seven years before. The wings were raked sharply at 35 degrees and, being located below the fuselage rather than on top of it as in the B-47 and the succeeding B-52, were angled upward to provide ground clearance for the pod-mounted engines. The main undercarriage consisted of two trucks, each with four wheels, that retracted inward from the wing toward the centerline. The new shape was to form the fundamental blueprint for successive Boeing jetliners and created the foundation for the company family of modern jetliners.

Boeing also used the Dash 80 to mark the start of a new internal numbering system that had been adopted in 1951. Following the sequence perpetuated with the B-47 and B-52, which had model numbers up to 499, the company had allocated 500 up to 599 for industrial products then being produced. The numbers 600 to 699 were allotted to missiles, which Boeing was then becoming involved with. The new jetliner products were allotted numbers from 700 on, with the Dash 80 designated the 707. To the present day, no one has been able to explain why the first six numbers were skipped, but some say the designation was simply chosen for luck.

Whatever the case, good fortune certainly smiled on the new jetliner, which successfully attracted massive business from the U.S. Air Force as a tanker/transport and from the world's airlines. In all, more than 800 of the military tanker derivative (KC-135/C-135) were built, while eventual sales of the 707 reached 1,013—the first jetliner to exceed 1,000.

The 707 began to make its first real

impact as a modern jetliner with the availability of a newer type of jet engine, the Pratt & Whitney JT3D and Rolls-Royce Conway turbofans. Unlike the earlier Pratt & Whitney JT3A turbojets that originally powered the first versions, the newer engines had a modest bypass capability that increased power and yet reduced noise and fuel consumption. While sales of the Conway-powered 707-400 were sluggish, the JT3D completely transformed the popularity of the 707-300 Intercontinental version. Out of all

Boeing widened the 707 fuselage by a total of 16 inches to 12 feet, 4 inches overall, providing room for six-across seating and staving off competition from the DC-8. The increase was accommodated in the upper arc of the fuselage and faired into the smaller diameter arc of the lower section to create a smooth-contoured ellipse and the now-familiar Boeing "double-bubble" cross-section.

The tanker/transport "Dash 80" also gave birth to the Model 717, which was renamed the KC-135 by the U.S. Air Force. To prolong the life of its trusty tanker workhorses, the Air Force began re-engining them in 1982 with the more powerful, fuel-efficient CFM56 turbofan. The KC-135R, as the version was called, could off-load up to 65 percent more fuel and fly farther.

707/720s built, some 580 were –300s, while another 130 had similar features such as the longer fuselage, higher payload, and longer range.

LITTLE BOEINGS

Two years before 707 launch customer Pan American began commercial operations with the first 707 in October 1958, the company had already begun looking for the next member of the jetliner family. Spurred on by two huge U.S. airlines, Eastern and United, the manufacturer began studies of a jet-powered airliner for short to medium routes. Although the 720, a shortened version of the 707, had been developed as an interim, Boeing knew the real answer to the challenging economics of short-haul jetliner operations was in a new design.

The result was the 727, which was given project status in September 1959. The trijet used the same fuselage cross-section as the 707 but was otherwise radically new. It had a T-tail, three new Pratt & Whitney JT8D

engines clustered around the tail, and aerodynamically "clean" wings. Optimized for short field performance, the 727 was equally at home on long- or medium-length routes. The first version, dubbed the 727-100, made its maiden flight from Renton on February 9, 1963, and was followed within four years by a stretched variant, the –200. Just like the 707 before it, the advent of the –200 transformed the sales of the trijet. By 1982, when production ceased, 1,831 of all 727 models had been built. The 727 firmly established Boeing as the dominant supplier to the rapidly growing U.S. domestic jetliner market. Just as important, it opened up new markets and customer opportunities around the world and established Boeing's winning "jetliner family" formula.

The company took this one step further with the 737, the "baby" of Boeing's family until the adoption of the 717 in 1998 (see chapter 2). The little twinjet was Boeing's first true short-haul jetliner and was launched in November 1964 to compete

A rarely seen, short-bodied 707-138 takes off from Houston George Bush Intercontinental Airport, Texas. The aircraft was shortened to meet Qantas' needs for an increased range jetliner for its long-haul Pacific routes. Although only 13 were built in all, it proved Boeing's willingness to develop derivatives to meet market demand.

with two established players, the Douglas DC-9 and the British Aircraft Corporation (BAC) One Eleven. The early designs were also T-tailed, just like both the competing aircraft and its larger sister, the 727. The decision to retain the existing fuselage cross-section of both the 707 and 727, coupled with short fuselage of the new aircraft, convinced Boeing to opt instead for a conventional tail. This meant the engines had to be relocated to the traditional underwing location, despite the limited ground clearance.

The need for short field performance was thought to be crucial to the design, so the wing was given a relatively modest sweep (by Boeing standards) of only 25 degrees. It was also canted up by 6 degrees for ground clearance, increasing the depth of the wing

Pratt & Whitney's JT3D-7 turbofan transformed the performance of the 707, adding power, range, and payload. Note the open position of the engine's blow-in, auxiliary inlets on this Colombian registered freighter on takeoff from Miami. This -324C, which first flew in April 1967 destined for Continental Airlines, is fitted with a 91-by-134-inch forward cargo door and can carry up to 7,415 cubic feet on the upper deck.

advent of the 737-200 Advanced, that sales really picked up. The Advanced, which included several aerodynamic and systems improvements, helped push overall -200 sales to 1,114 by the time deliveries were completed in August 1988.

The biggest stimulus to the 737 came in 1980 when Boeing began looking at the newly developed medium thrust, high-bypass ratio engines then entering development. In March 1981, it launched the 737-300 when Southwest Airlines and USAir ordered 10 each. All were powered by the CFM International CFM56, marking the start of one of the most successful engine-airframe partnerships in jetliner history.

The extra power of the CFM56 also meant the basic aircraft could be stretched. The result was an overall length increase to 109 feet, 7 inches and seating for up to 149. A further stretch, dubbed the -400, was launched in June 1986 with an order for 25 from Piedmont Airlines. The 737-400 was 120 inches longer than the -300, making it just 5 inches shorter than the venerable Dash 80. The longer 737 could also seat up to 171 passengers, thereby eclipsing other embryonic Boeing projects in that seat category such as the 7J7. The baseline -300 was also later shrunk to produce what was effectively a 130-seat 737-200 replacement. The resulting 737-500 was 101 feet, 9 inches long and was launched with orders and options for 73 aircraft in May 1987 from Braathens SAFE, Euralair, Maersk, and Southwest.

The low operating costs, high reliability, and good performance of the re-engined 737 family brought huge sales success, and by the mid-1990s, the little twin was the best-selling jetliner in history.

TWIN-AISLE REVOLUTION

Boeing owes its dominance of the jetliner industry to the mighty 747, which emerged in the 1960s from the ashes of a failed military air-lifter bid. The two designs, one for a massive Air Force cargo aircraft, the other for a trunk line passenger and freighter aircraft, are not linked, but they share common origins.

The unusual T-tail trijet configuration of the 727 is emphasized in this close up of the aft section of this UPS-operated -100. UPS opted to re-engine its -100 fleet with the Rolls-Royce Tay 650, which required more airflow and therefore larger intakes. Most other surviving -100s and -200s were either hushkitted or fitted with other aerodynamic modifications to comply with early 2000 noise regulations.

and creating an exceptional fuel capacity. This was to play a big part in extending the range, and therefore the life of the 737 for many years to come.

Despite early structural problems with the wing and development issues with the engine and its thrust-reverser design, the 737-100 attracted interest from Lufthansa, which launched it into life with an order for 22 in February 1965. It was the first Boeing jetliner to be launched by a non-U.S. operator.

It quickly became apparent to Boeing that it would attract more interest with a slightly larger derivative, the -200. This was 6 feet, 6 inches longer than the -100, giving it an overall length of just more than 100 feet and providing room for up to 130 passengers. Despite the stretch, sales slowed rather than speeded up, and it was not until the

The engineering concepts and know-how that allowed an aircraft of the scale of the 747 to be built were learned by Boeing during its attempt to win the Air Force's CX-HLS (cargo experimental–heavy logistics system) competition. The other essential piece of the jigsaw that fell into place as a result of the CX-HLS was the development of huge, new high-bypass ratio turbofans by GE and Pratt & Whitney. Again,

the 747 benefited from this competition, but used the Pratt & Whitney JT9D engine, which lost out to the GE engine for the military contract.

The stimulus for the 747 came from Pan American, which wanted a bigger-capacity aircraft to cope with surging passenger demand on key routes around the world, particularly across the north Atlantic. Boeing studied stretches of the 707 to match those of

The sophisticated high-lift devices at the leading and trailing edges of the 727 wing are clearly visible in this view of an American Airlines -200 on climb out. American kept a large number of its -200s in service beyond 2000 by either modifying them with aerodynamic kits developed by Raisbeck, or by fitting them with FedEx-developed hushkits.

Low evening sunlight catches a Boeing 720 in storage at Mojave, California. The 720 was soon eclipsed by the 727 and was destined for a short production life. This 720-060B was built in 1965 and flew for Ethiopian Airlines, MEA, and others before eventually becoming an advanced sensor testbed for Hughes Aircraft, later Raytheon E-Systems. Note the unusual side-mounted sensor window near the wing root.

Lufthansa launched the 737 and maintained a long relationship with the little twinjet. This -230 first flew as late as 1980 and was one of more than 100 737s eventually operated by the German flag-carrier. Note the absence of any folding doors for the undercarriage wheels. These were omitted from the original design for weight and cost reasons and, to this day, the 737 remains the only Boeing jetliner built with exposed main wheels.

The world's most faithful 737 operator is, without doubt, Southwest Airlines. The Texas-based airline was an all-737-200 operator when it launched the -300 in March 1981. It later helped launch the 737-500 and, in November 1993, launched the Next Generation 737-700.

the DC-8, but failed to make any economic sense of the results. After losing the CX-HLS contract, in 1965 it set up a project office to design a huge new aircraft around the bigger engines that were now becoming available.

To Boeing's surprise, the airlines, particularly Pan Am, wanted the aircraft to be as big as possible.

After wrestling with more than 200 outline concepts, Boeing began to narrow down the field to several double-deck designs and one finalist with a single, wide deck. This latter design was heavily influenced by the strategic thinkers within Pan Am and Boeing who predicted that most long-haul traffic would soon become the domain of the supersonic transports (SSTs) also in development by then. The new design, they argued, would be far more useful if it could be readily converted into a freighter when the time came to change over to SSTs.

The baseline 747 cross-section was therefore drawn up around two sea-going 8-by-8-foot containers side by side on a single wide deck. The flight deck was put out of the way, on top of the fuselage, to allow the entire nose to hinge in order to provide access to the cargo deck. Although hardly conscious of the fact at the time, Boeing had just created the world's first wide-body transport and set the scene for the most fundamental step change in aerospace since the birth of the jet engine.

The program was launched in December 1965 when Pan Am signed a letter of intent for 25 at the then staggering price of $20 million a copy. Boeing's commitment was even greater as it had been forced to pump an astronomic $1 billion into the program and the development of a huge new facility at Everett, north of Seattle, in which to build the monstrous new aircraft.

The 747, which outwardly resembled a scaled-up 707 in basic configuration, was rolled out for the first time on September 30, 1968. It was 231 feet, 4 inches long and had a span of 195 feet, 8 inches, making it by far the largest civil airliner in the world and the second largest aircraft after the Lockheed C-5A Galaxy that had won the original air-lifter contest. It made its maiden flight on February 9, 1969, and, after overcoming the first phase of a troublesome initial period with its new engines, was certified for service in December that year.

The initial -100 ordered by Pan Am and the bulk of the world's largest airlines provided the basis for several successive generations, the first of which was the heavier -200. Designated the -200B, it was structurally beefed-up with thicker skins, stringers, landing gear beams, flaps, and ribs. It was also the first to benefit from higher thrust engines, which were to pace the development of the 747 from then on. The availability of competing powerplants from General Electric and Rolls-Royce added to the commercial success of the -200, which quickly overtook

the -100's order book. In all, some 393 -200 versions were sold, compared to 205 -100s, including some specially developed domestic 100SR (short range) models for Japan

The long-awaited stretch version, which was confidently planned into the original design from day one, seemed elusive, and the nearest Boeing got to it during the first two decades of the program was with the -300. This involved a stretch of the upper deck only, providing room for a maximum of 91 passengers in all economy—a far cry from the original design, which had seating for just three passengers. The hump was extended aft 23 feet, 4 inches, providing seating for 44 more than the -200B. Despite the improved capacity, the range was no greater. As a result, the -300 was only a moderate success, with only 81 sold.

This was good compared to the shortened 747SP, a long-haul variant that was cut down in size by 48 feet, 4 inches to trade weight for range. The growing capability of Boeing's own 747-200 and the emergence of more cost-effective trijet and later twinjet competitors meant the 747SP's niche closed

The CFM56 engine totally transformed the fortunes of the 737 from the launch of the -300 in 1981. Nineteen years later, more than 2,000 CFM56-powered Classics had been sold. A late production -300 operated by Virgin Express here leads a British Midland -400 at London Heathrow. Note the flattened lower lip of the intake to increase ground clearance.

One of the most famous aircraft-airline associations in civil jetliner history. The 747 was largely conceived, developed, and launched around the requirements of Pan American and its ebullient chairman Juan Trippe. One of the airline's earliest 747-100s, appropriately called Clipper Juan Trippe, is pictured here taxiing for takeoff at Heathrow's runway 9 Right shortly before the airline's collapse in 1991. This veteran aircraft, line number two, first flew in April 1969 and served the airline from October 1970 onward.

up as quickly as it opened, condemning it to being the shortest production run of any significant Boeing jetliner variant.

The first three main generations of the 747 nonetheless played a pivotal role in establishing Boeing as the supreme jetliner champion. It raised the stakes for all other manufacturers, eventually forcing Lockheed out of the civil business altogether after huge losses with its L-1011 TriStar program. The pursuit of wide-body success, also sparked by Boeing's initiative, triggered Douglas into developing the DC-10, which was eventually completed under the stewardship of the combined McDonnell Douglas company. It also raised the bar so significantly for other European manufacturers that they were forced to join together as the Airbus consortium in order to produce an indigenous wide-body design.

NEW TECHNOLOGY TWINS

Boeing reached a watershed in the late 1970s as it began defining two new-generation aircraft at virtually the same time. Although both were aimed at significantly different marketplaces, the close timing eventually persuaded Boeing to develop them concurrently, thereby treating the two as almost a single program. Although the two therefore began life in different directions, they ended up sharing similar aerodynamic, structural, and system features as well as identical flight decks. The tale is even more remarkable given that one aircraft, the 757, was a narrow-body—or single aisle—aircraft, while the 767 was a wide-body and only the company's second twin-aisle design after the 747.

The 757 emerged out of studies aimed at replacing the 727-200. Although United and

others were interested in a proposed stretch of the -200, the 727-300, they quickly lost interest when they discovered Boeing was studying an advanced development project dubbed the 7N7. The main aim of the project, like a parallel effort dubbed the 7X7, was to capture a new wave of materials, design, and propulsion technology sweeping into the civil aerospace industry. The advances, par-

ticularly in the new engines, were of great interest to the airlines, which had seen fuel prices rise from $0.11 per U.S. gallon to more than $1.10 within a few months after the Yom Kippur Middle East War of 1973.

Reduced weight, advanced aerodynamics, and a slim fuselage led Boeing toward estimates of 40 percent fuel savings on a 1,000-nautical mile trip versus the 727-200.

The inherent flexibility of the 747's basic design gave it the ability to keep growing to meet constant airline demand for more range and payload. Until the -400, the most successful of all these growth versions was the -200, of which 393 were delivered over 21 years. The -200 was the first 747 version to be offered with an engine choice as illustrated here by this Rolls-Royce powered British Airways aircraft. The first RB.211-524 powered 747 was delivered to British Airways on June 16, 1977.

The stretched upper deck of the -300 helped increase the maximum passenger capacity of the 747 to an amazing 580 in all-economy. French airline UTA took delivery of the first all-passenger -300 on March 1, 1983. One of the airline's -300's, appropriately called "Big Boss," is pictured being towed at Charles de Gaulle airport, Paris.

The 7N7 concept was firmed up into two major versions by 1978. Both would be single-aisle, twin-engined aircraft with advanced, but moderately swept wings and a slim-line version of the 727 tail arrangement. The 7N7-100 had seats for around 160 and the second, dubbed the -200, was configured for 180 seats and up. At this stage, the 7N7 still had the 727 forward fuselage and flight deck. One of the key new features, however, was the advanced wing design. The 7N7 was the first Boeing concept to come to fruition with an aft-loaded wing in which lift was produced across most of the upper surface, rather than across a relatively narrow band close behind the leading edge. The new, deeper wing was far more efficient throughout the speed range, produced less drag, and held more fuel within its cavernous structure. Lift performance was so good, in fact, that an elaborate set of flaps, slats, and spoilers were designed to enable it to be "slowed down" effectively from cruise to landing.

The 7N7 gradually evolved away from any links with the 727 as the design encompassed more and more advances in structures and systems. The T-tail disappeared quite late in the program, finally vanishing in favor of a conventional tail almost a year after the two launch customers, Eastern and British Airways, announced their intent to place orders. These were duly placed in March 1979 when the two carriers signed for a total of 40 aircraft, which were now formally called the 757. The aircraft would be powered by the Rolls-Royce RB.211-535C engine, marking the first time a Boeing jetliner had been launched with a nondomestic engine. The rival Pratt & Whitney PW2000 was launched on the aircraft in November 1980, when Delta placed a massive order for 60 757s. The first 757 made its maiden flight on February 19, 1982, and entered service with Eastern on New Year's Day 1983. The first Pratt & Whitney-powered 757 flew almost a year later and was delivered to Delta on November 5, 1984.

Meanwhile, the 767 was emerging slowly from the complex studies that went back to 1972 with the formation of the 7X7 organization. Airlines were ambiguous about

their exact requirements, which called for a "semi-wide-body" that fit in somewhere between the 707 and DC-10. At the same time, Boeing used the 7X7 to expand in other new directions. From early on, the company involved Italy's Aeritalia along with a consortium of Japanese aerospace companies as a way of spreading development costs and encouraging international sales.

In 1976 major decisions were finalized over the number of engines and the whole direction of the program. The priority was switched from a proposed trijet version to the twinjet. As the 7X7 was always going to be a wide-body, the decision represented something of a milestone for Boeing. Airbus had pioneered the wide-bodied twin concept with the A300B and with Boeing's adoption of the twin as the number one choice, this reflected an acknowledgment

that the new generation engines were both reliable and more economical.

The 7X7 finally became the 767 by 1978 when three major variants were on the table. They included a 190-seat 767-100, a larger 210-seat 767-200, and a trijet version dubbed the 767MR/LR. This 200-seater was designated for the intercontinental routes but soon disappeared altogether as the twinjet solution took over. The 767MR/LR was later briefly termed the 777 before its role was assumed by a new, extended-range version of the 767-200, dubbed the -200ER.

On July 14, 1978, the 767 was finally launched by United, which ordered 30 series -200s powered by Pratt & Whitney JT9Ds. Later that year, American and Delta both ordered the General Electric CF6-80A-powered version, signifying the fact that the 767 was the first Boeing jetliner launched

Eastern Airlines launched the 757 with British Airways with combined orders for 40 in 1979. Unusually it opted to retain elements of the Boeing demonstrator livery in its own paint scheme, the "757" titling being evident here on the tail of this early aircraft seen departing Miami 11 years later.

The "semi-wide-body" fuselage of the 767, seen clearly in this view of an American Airlines aircraft, gave it a maximum cabin width of 15 feet, 6 inches. This provided room for up to seven-abreast seating, but reduced the impact of drag on the design, which was aimed at the gap between the 727 and DC-10.

with a choice of engines. The first 767 rolled out at Everett on August 4, 1981, to reveal its large, 156-foot, 1-inch wingspan, low tailplane, and widely spaced undercarriage.

Boeing was particularly proud of the wing, which reached new levels with the 767 design. The wing was swept at 31.5 degrees, slightly more than the 757, which was optimized for long-range cruise at Mach 0.8. The advanced aerodynamics of the aft-loaded wing gave the best spanwise distribution of lift ever achieved on a Boeing jetliner to that date. The thickness of the new wing also ensured plenty of room for fuel, an important feature that was to serve the aircraft in largely unexpected ways over its career.

The relatively late change to a standard, low-tail design instead of the T-tail had been made because it allowed more passengers to be carried without increasing aircraft length. The unusual, seven-abreast cross-section also enabled Boeing to taper the rear fuselage in a shorter length which, in turn, meant parallel walls along the entire passenger cabin length.

United began commercial service with the first 767 on September 8, 1982, between

Chicago and Denver while the first GE-powered 767 entered service with Delta on December 15. Two months later, Boeing announced the go-ahead of a stretched model, the 767-300. The new stretch increased overall length by 21 feet to 132 feet, 5 inches, with a 121-inch plug in the forward fuselage and a 132-inch plug aft. First orders for the -300 were placed by JAL in September 1983; Delta followed the next February. Boeing's decision to expand the 767 was virtually inevitable, given the capacity of the baseline design, the height of the undercarriage, and the size of the wing. The -300 gave a huge boost to 767 sales, and by early 1999 around 580 aircraft, or more than two-thirds of all 767s ordered, were the longer version.

The first -300 flew in January 1976 and entered service later that year. Like the -200 before it, the -300ER quickly followed, leading to a dramatic spread of international 767 operations on long-haul routes. Boeing also followed up with a Rolls-Royce RB.211-524G/H–powered version and, in 1993, began development of a 767-300F freighter version for the United Parcel Service (UPS).

The development followed a similar exercise for UPS which, in late 1985, ordered the first of up to 75 special package freighter versions of the 757-200.

The 757 and 767 were unique in Boeing jetliner history in that they were the first to share common flight decks and handling qualities. The initiative was taken because both were twinjets, with similarly configured systems, and both were in concurrent development. The move would therefore enable crews to obtain a common type rating, reducing crew training, simplifying scheduling, and allowing airlines flying both types to adopt a common seniority roster. The company also hoped that common instrumentation, avionics, and systems would cut the cost and time of certification. Both were also the first new Boeing flight decks to be designed from the outset without a flight engineer. Though provision was initially retained for a third crew member, the basic concept was for a two-crew cockpit with a greater degree of automation, display flexibility, and simpler systems management.

The key to this was new TV-type cathode-ray tube (CRT) screens developed by Rockwell Collins. Six screens were used: two electronic flight instrumentation system (EFIS) displays for each pilot and a shared pair of engine indication and crew alerting system (EICAS) displays. The EFIS replaced the original electromechanical instruments while the EICAS replaced engine monitoring instruments and provided warning and caution messages. The screens could also be used to check the status of aircraft systems, thereby playing the role of flight engineer.

The 757 and 767 were also given an enhanced version of the "brain" that had been introduced with the 747 in the form of a flight management system (FMS). This linked the air-data computer, autopilot, inertial reference navigation system, thrust management computer, and caution/warning system. It allowed navigation, performance management, and automatic flight to be controlled through a single unit, dramatically reducing pilot workload.

The new twins therefore synthesized a comprehensive leap in technology that would provide the platform for an entirely new set of modern Boeing jetliners.

By the late 1990s some of the earlier production 767-200s were enjoying new lives as freighters. This aircraft was one of the first to be converted for Airborne Express from a batch of 12 bought from Japanese carrier All Nippon Airways.

CHAPTER TWO

717:
BACK TO
THE FUTURE

The smallest member of the modern Boeing jetliner family is, perhaps, the most surprising of all. The 717, once known as the MD-95, is the last survivor of the McDonnell Douglas product line taken over by Boeing in 1997.

The 717 came close to not surviving. The program started painfully slow, seemed to die several times before birth, and was close to cancellation on numerous occasions. Threatened by Boeing's 737-600 before the takeover, it then faced the threat of extinction after the merger, as Boeing considered its future strategy. The fate of the 717 hung by a thread until Airbus decided to develop the AE31X regional jet with Asia, prompting Boeing to look again at the MD-95.

T-2 lifts off from Yuma on another test flight. Note the large, 58-inch-diameter intakes of the BR715 engines. Tests revealed a significantly lower than expected fuel burn.

The first production 717-200, P-1 comes together for AirTran in October 1998. By now the full impact of the Boeing takeover was being felt at Long Beach as evidenced in the far background by the once unthinkable sight of 737s inside Building 80. The Next Generation 737s were formerly used in the certification program and required refurbishing before delivery.

outlined a study aircraft called the DC-9-90. This was a short-bodied version of the DC-9-81, which later became the MD-81. The small twinjet was aimed at the newly deregulated U.S. airline market and could seat 117. By the mid-1980s, the DC-9-90 study was superseded by the MD-87. This very different, heavier aircraft formed the foundation for Douglas' next stab at the 100-seater market in the shape of the MD-87-105. The -105 was 8 feet shorter than the MD-87 and was aimed at the DC-9-30 replacement market, in general, and Northwest Airlines, in particular.

The American airline had a deep interest in the DC-9 and its replacement, particularly since it operated the world's largest fleet of the old Douglas twinjet. Northwest Airlines therefore became closely involved with Douglas on the project, which gradually evolved into a firm program with a new name: the MD-95. The designation was first used at the 1991 Paris air show where McDonnell Douglas, Pratt & Whitney, and the China National Aero-Technology Import Export (CATIC) agency signed a memorandum of understanding to develop a 105-seater. The aircraft, at this stage, was still based on a development of the MD-80, rather than the lighter DC-9 airframe, and

After surviving these threats, the 717 went on to face a pitched battle with the Airbus A318, which emerged from the ashes of the AE31X proposal and was eventually launched by Airbus in April 1999. This sturdy little T-tail twinjet therefore defied the odds to survive again and again and went on to enter service in mid-1999, providing Boeing with a valuable foot in the door of the regional market.

The story of the 717 goes back to 1983 when Douglas Aircraft Company, the commercial arm of McDonnell Douglas,

The second test 717-200, T-2, takes shape in Building 80 at Long Beach in January 1998 with a T-3 in the adjacent position. The background is dominated by MD-80s and MD-90s, the latter of which were mostly destined for Saudi Arabian Airlines. Note the hastily attached fuselage titles, which only a few days before, had read "MD-95."

was timed for initial deliveries in 1995, hence the designation MD-95.

At this stage, the MD-95 had closer links with both the MD-90 and the Chinese Trunkliner program, both of which were now underway. The concept therefore looked more like the original DC-9-90 than the DC-9-30, to which it later gravitated. A key element of the proposal was a more fuel-efficient engine with Stage 3 capability. The MD-95 was offered with either the JT8D-218, a larger fanned version of the JT8D, which had become the standard MD-80 powerplant, or the Rolls-Royce Tay 670. First flight was scheduled for 1994, but the fast-track development was derailed by the sudden recession of the early 1990s.

In desperation, Douglas decided to aim its twinjet development plans at an extensive upgrade of the existing DC-9. The DC-9X included major upgrades of the cabin, flight deck, systems, and engines. Although the DC-9X ultimately came to nothing, it at least provided an opening for a little-known newcomer to the engine world, BMW Rolls-Royce. The Anglo-German engine company was established to develop the BR700, a new technology family aimed at the high-end corporate jet and regional airliner family. The BR710 version, the first member of the new jet family, was selected for two long-range bizjets, Bombardier's Global Express and Gulfstream's GV, while the DC-9X was considered an option to launch the higher thrust BR715.

By 1994, there were signs of a recovery in the market so Douglas began to revive the MD-95 once again. This time the delay benefited BMW Rolls-Royce and Douglas Aircraft Company. They could now offer a new technology engine for a revised, light-weight design. Douglas had shifted its priority back to the DC-9-30 type design rather than the MD-87. By July 1994, Douglas got the McDonnell Douglas board approval to offer the aircraft produced through a unique risk and revenue partnership, with a network of suppliers around the world. Douglas, by this stage, was beginning to suffer from its lack of investment in other siblings for the twin and trijet families. Confidence in the future of the company was low and, without

Pictured within 48 hours of first flight, T-1 is readied for another set of engine ground runs. The 717 made an unusual site in Boeing house colors on the former Douglas delivery ramp, but by bringing it into the Boeing line-up, the enlarged company hoped the twinjet would live up to its name and literally start "Bringing People Together." BELOW: The clamshell thrust reverser, isogrid casing, and "easy access" cowling of the BMW Rolls-Royce BR715 engine are clearly displayed as tests continue in the run-up to first flight in late August 1998.

High-tech combustion systems and a high-bypass-ratio design helped the 717 become one of the most environmentally friendly jetliners ever made. As well as being exceptionally quiet, the engines burned cleaner, producing 80 percent fewer hydrocarbons, 70 percent fewer emissions of carbon monoxide, and around 42 percent less smoke than the limits set by ICAO's international rules. RIGHT: After several months of delays caused by system and engine-related issues, first flight finally took place on a hot September 2, 1998. The aircraft landed at the Boeing test facility in Yuma, Arizona, after a 4-hour and 10-minute maiden flight from Long Beach.

the risk-sharing arrangement devised to launch the MD-95, it is doubtful that the project would have started at all.

Major suppliers included Alenia, Douglas' faithful Italian supplier and partner on so many projects, Halla (later Hyundai of South Korea), Korean Air, and the Aero Industry Development Center of Taiwan (which took empennage work originally awarded to British Aerospace). To pare costs to a minimum, and frustrated by punitive environmental legislation at its home base in Long Beach, California, Douglas made the unusual decision to site final assembly out of state. Dalfort Aviation's Dallas site in Texas was the chosen place, though this ultimately reverted to Long Beach after hard bargaining with the unions and concessions from the California state government and local utility companies. Total development costs at the time were estimated at around $500 million, of which some $200 million was directly payable by Douglas Aircraft Company.

With everything in order, all Douglas Aircraft Company needed was a launch customer. Price was the key to several competitions waged, with the Next Generation 737-600 and slightly larger Airbus A319 as the main challengers. All industry eyes were on a hard-fought competition in Scandinavia

for an SAS fleet requirement. SAS ranked with KLM as one of the most loyal Douglas customers, and it was widely expected that the Scandinavian flag carrier would look favorably on the MD-95. But times were different and Boeing came in with an aggressive last-minute price that Douglas was unable to match. The industry was shocked therefore when, on March 14, 1995, SAS placed orders and options for 70 Boeing 737-600s.

The loss proved almost fatal to the MD-95 and sent confidence in Douglas' future down to an all-time low. The sales team battled on and, on October 19, 1995, announced the news that the Douglas workforce had been waiting for—a launch order for 50 plus 50 options. The deal was secured with low-price American carrier ValuJet, which was establishing itself as a southeastern version of Texas-based Southwest Airlines. Still, questions remained. No further orders were collected and the future of both Douglas and ValuJet, which changed its name to AirTran after suffering a fatal accident in Florida in 1996, continued to seem uncertain.

Then came the Boeing takeover. Douglas Aircraft Company's Seattle competitor fought tooth and nail to beat the MD-95 with the 737-600, so it seemed

highly unlikely Boeing would elect to continue with the program. Most pundits expected the company to close down the line after delivering the aircraft it was under contract to supply to AirTran. In November 1997, Boeing announced it was shutting down the MD-80 and MD-90 lines, but reserved judgment on the MD-11 and MD-95. Again, the Long Beach team held its breath.

Then, in January 1998, Boeing announced the fate of the MD-95 at a press conference in Long Beach. Over the holiday break Boeing's strategic development and marketing people had decided that the virtually ready-made MD-95 could compete in the regional market with greater speed than anything Airbus could produce. Discussions between Airbus and several Asian countries over the development of a proposed AE31X regional jet had dragged on for months, but this posed a significant threat nonetheless. Furthermore, the potential market in the 90–120 seat category could not be ignored. Boeing estimated this category to be around 2,100 aircraft over 20 years, much of it made up of DC-9 replacement requirements.

The decision was therefore made, not just to keep the MD-95, but to rename it the 717-200. (The –100 and –300 designations were reserved for potential 80- and 120-seat derivatives previously known as the MD-95-20 and MD-95-50.) The 717 title took most people by surprise. It had originally been assigned (as the 717-100A) to the first 29 KC-135A tankers ordered by the U.S. Air Force in the 1950s. Later, the 717 was briefly assigned to the medium-range 707-020 derivative. This eventually emerged as the 720 (see chapter 1), and this time Boeing justified the use of the title to denote its first purpose-made 100-seater. It also offered the company a chance to symbolically tie in the last remaining Douglas product as one of its own and, in doing so, Boeing hoped that market confidence in the future of the product would be assuaged.

INSIDE THE 717

From the outside, the most striking impression of the 717 was the size of the engines. With a fan diameter of 58 inches, the fuselage-mounted BR715s produced an almost disproportionate look. The engine's 24 solid titanium, wide-chord fan blades were driven by a 2-stage high-pressure turbine and a 10-stage high-pressure compressor derived from International Aero Engines' V2500. The

T-1 was soon racking up test hours from Yuma and is pictured here on rotation for yet another sortie a little over a month after first flight. Note the extended fin tip cap and fully deflected elevators.

Maximum power takeoff and climb out tests were performed with the gear deliberately kept down to produce drag and "keep it on the back of the drag curve," while maintaining constant V2 (positive climb speed). Note the extended trailing static cone, which was used for collecting data to calibrate the aircraft's onboard flight instruments, and the orange-colored cap over the antispin chute housing.

BR715 was also fitted with a 2-stage low-pressure compressor and a 3-stage low-pressure turbine. The engine ran for the first time in its BR715 configuration on April 28, 1997, and was throttled up to its redline limit of 25,745 pounds of thrust during initial tests.

From the airline aspect, the key feature of the engine was its ease of maintenance. After input from an airline advisory team, the pneumatics were located on top of the engine and fuel and oil access areas at the base. The engine was mounted on simple, long-duct nacelles that provided easy maintenance access to components in the fan case. The hinged lower door was strong enough to support two engineers and their maintenance equipment. The BR715 was also fitted with an electronic engine control (EEC) to extend engine life and provide automated fault reporting and close monitoring. The EEC eliminated the need for throttle rigging during engine change and allowed many components to be changed without the engine verification run needed on the DC-9.

The other small, tail-mounted engine, the Sundstrand APIC (Auxiliary Power International) APS2100 APU was also equipped with an electronic control unit. The APU inlet was moved from the lower aft section to the upper left side of the fuselage to reduce noise on the ramp to workable levels. The 717 was the first program in which Sundstrand Power Systems was responsible for more than just the APU itself. As well as the APS2100, it designed and was responsible for certifying the inlet duct, inlet door, exhaust duct, and support frame assembly.

In common with the powerplants, the systems were also designed to be low maintenance and basically trouble-free. The primary electrical system, for example, consisted of three identical power conversion and distribution units (PCDUs). These performed the functions formerly provided by a generator control unit in conjunction with the transformer rectifier and bus tie relays. "All three are the same and effectively give us a hot spare," said 717 chief project engineer, Tom

Croslin. "Two are OK for dispatch on the minimum equipment list, which is ideal if you have a problem and you are out in the middle of nowhere." The system consisted of two engine-mounted, 35/40-kilovolt ampere integrated-drive generators and a 60-kilovolt ampere APU generator. Each was controlled by a PCDU. The primary electrical relays were modular and mounted to the front of the PCDU for easy replacement.

The fuel system was an improved version of the original DC-9 layout with a more reliable quantity gauging system and the addition of pressure sensors on each pump. Optional auxiliary tanks have been designed for installation during an overnight shift. Standard fuel capacity was 3,673 U.S. gallons and could be increased with the optional 565-gallon tanks. The pneumatic and ice protection systems were simplified, thanks to the use of a single isolation valve instead of dual cross-feeds. This allowed simultaneous anti-icing of the wing and horizontal stabilizer leading edges. "Rather than having alternating protection on the surfaces, we've made two significant improvements. We had shared flow under the old design in which we would bleed air for 15 minutes on the wings and 2.5 minutes on the tail. Now with this split system we

get simultaneous protection. We believed the regulations were moving towards more stringent requirements, particularly with it being a T-tailed design," Croslin added.

Flight test engineers restow an antispin chute in the specially designed tail canister of T-1 in the early evening before sunset after a day of stall testing in the Bakersfield area of California. More than 200 stall maneuvers were carried out by Boeing without a hitch before many of the tests were repeated for certification by the FAA and JAA.

Tufts were attached to the empennage and engine pylons to visualize aerodynamic flow in cruise and slow-speed flight conditions. The behavior of the tufts, like tell-tales on the sail of a yacht, gave clear and instant indications of airflow patterns over the skin surface. Early performance tests showed encouraging signs that drag and fuel burn were "nominal or better" according to Boeing.

Another device called PODS (or pneumatic overheat detection system), provided a backup to the valve system and eliminated the tail and wing de-icing timers and relays. To improve the reliability of PODS, dual loop sensors replaced bimetallic point sensors used on the original design. If it detected a leak, or a burst, the affected part was automatically shut off. The "piccolo" tube that distributed bleed air to the leading edge of the stabilizer was extended to the tips.

The 717 also incorporated an advanced air-conditioning pack made by AlliedSignal. This used a "three-wheel" arrangement in which the connecting shaft between the air conditioning unit's existing two wheels was extended to run a third. The same power was therefore used to pull in exterior air over the heat exchanger, eliminating the need for a dedicated cooling fan. The air was fed into a new-look cabin crafted by interior specialist Fischer of Austria. Complete with improved lighting, larger overhead storage bins, new three-bay sidewall panels, and modular lavatories with a vacuum waste system, the interior was a world away from the original DC-9.

In common with virtually all the recent Boeing (and Douglas) flight decks, the 717 was dominated by six 8-inch-by-8-inch, liquid crystal, flat panel displays. The screens were driven by two Honeywell-made versatile integrated avionics (VIA) computers, which form the heart and brain of the flight deck. Not only did the VIAs run the screens, they also functioned as the flight management system, central aural warning system, and flight data acquisition system. The three left-hand displays were normally driven by VIA number one and the three right-hand screens by VIA number two; however, either VIA could drive all six if needed.

Screens one and six were used mainly as primary flight displays, while numbers two and five were used for navigation displays. The number three screen was used for the

engine and alert display, while the remaining screen, number four, was used as a systems display. This included synoptic display of several systems including air, fuel, hydraulics, engines, electrical, and configuration of the aircraft. This last display presented a view of the 717 looking forward from behind the aircraft. All control surfaces, ailerons, rudder, elevators, flaps, slats, and spoilers were shown pictorially. Landing gear indicators provided a backup display of the landing gear position as well as providing the temperatures of individual brakes.

Flight guidance consisted of two flight control computers (FCCs) and a glare shield control panel adapted from the MD-11. The FCCs provided autopilot, autothrottle, flight directors, stall warning, wind shear detection and guidance, and engine synchronization and provided the 717 with full Category IIIa autoland capability. A jump to Category IIIb was provisioned with the addition of a radio altimeter, instrument landing system receiver, and an inertial reference unit.

SOLID STRUCTURE

The largest area of structural change compared to the DC-9 was around the tail area. Much was due to the use of the heavier BR715 engines, which weighed up to 6,450 pounds (including nacelle) compared to

4,670 pounds for the original JT8D-7/9. To support the extra weight, Douglas designed an extra frame that was inserted between the existing aft frames. Thrust loads were taken on the front mount of the engine. "It was determined that it was better to take the loads straight in and cantilever the engines off the mount. Simplicity was the name of the game," said Croslin. The tail area used thicker skins and the hinge points were also beefed-up to meet new structural requirements for jammed control surfaces," added Croslin.

The fin shape looked a lot different, but that was because the overall design of the empennage was based on the MD-87. The unusual fin tip cap, a distinguishing feature of the -87, was made even more pronounced in the case of the 717 by extending it an extra 10 inches. This helped increase the static stability of the relatively stubby aircraft. To balance the heavier tail, the forward fuselage was stretched by three frames, or 57 inches. Careful attention was paid to ensure that this did not encroach on the 737, which of course, at the time, was still the competition. As Croslin recalled, "This played us right into perfect balance, though we were a little concerned at the time that we might be making the airplane too big. We didn't want to push ourselves onto the 737."

Work to prepare T-1 for its next sortie goes on into the evening as an engineer works on the antispin chute. Note the trailing cone.

cent was not changed. The wing was fitted with a series of drag improvements originally developed for Swissair's DC-9 fleet, and subsequent modifications were made for the MD-90 aerofoil. These included slat seals between ribs at the top and bottom of the slats. A redesigned fillet was also added to the wing-body join area and, together with the other wing improvements, was expected to yield a 1 percent drag benefit.

The fillet is one of the few composite parts of the aircraft. "The goal was not to use composites because the maintenance community hates it," said Croslin. "With composites you need things like autoclaves to repair it, whereas any farm boy from Minnesota can repair a dent in aluminum with a silver dollar patch." Other composite parts include the tip cap, aileron and elevator tabs, radome, wing trailing edge panels, and the low drag tail cone. Douglas took the opportunity to shift to more modern alloys developed over the intervening 30 years. This included the 2024T3 alloy used throughout much of the structure.

FLIGHT TEST

Preparations for rollout and first flight reached fever pitch in the first few months of 1998. The first of three test airframes, T-1, was essentially complete by the end of 1997 and awaited the fitting of the first engine ship sets, which arrived the following February from Rohr (now part of BFGoodrich) in San Diego.

Then, just as the schedule looked good for an on-time first flight, Boeing received some bad news from BMW Rolls-Royce. Altitude chamber tests revealed unexpected cracks in third-stage high-pressure compressor blades. Although Boeing and the engine maker knew the BR715s already installed on T-1 could be flown, even with this potential condition, neither wanted to take the chance and work on designing, testing, and retrofitting. A fix began immediately.

While the solution, which involved changes to the blades and variable stator scheduling system, was worked out, there was more bad news. The fan containment

The wing was essentially unchanged from that of the DC-9-30 family. The wing selected, because of the higher weight target of the 717, was that of the DC-9-34. The wing incidence angle, as on the -34, was raised by 1.25 degrees to increase maximum takeoff weight capability to 121,000 pounds. Area remained unaltered at 1,000.7 square feet, and the thickness/chord ratio of 11.6 per-

case, which absorbed the energy of any fan blades should they become dislodged, showed cracks after a fan blade was deliberately detached in a fan rig test that May. The case had to be redesigned with thicker aluminum and weight suffered as a result. "The blade itself was mostly contained, but we had a little fragment come out at low energy, and we decided to increase the thickness over the impact area," said Norbert Arndt, head of the BR715 project. Jim Phillips, the 717 program manager said the extra weight penalty was "still within the contingency envelope" and added that Boeing "still feels good about it." The combined engine problems meant a three-month delay to first flight.

Indeed, Phillips was surprisingly philosophical about the problems, given the pressure he and his team were under to get the aircraft flying, in the hope it would help promote sales. "One of the problems is when you have an engine development program pacing an aircraft program, you always have the chance of some setbacks. When we began looking at this we realized there was no existing engine capable of meeting the emissions, noise, and efficiency targets. The only engine that could meet them had not been developed, and we knew it was a risk, so I'm not surprised about a few months' delay. All in all we are amazingly close to where we thought we'd be at this stage," he added.

The engines were not the only culprits. Other "integration issues" had developed with the sophisticated new flight management system and electrically signaled spoilers. The FMS problem was essentially a software glitch within the VIA, whereas the spoiler problem centered on the discovery of a rare failure condition that could have resulted in inadvertent deployment. "There were a couple of areas where [we] went back to redesign them because, in isolated situations, there was a chance of inadvertent deployment," confirmed Phillips at the time.

While the aircraft waited for flight-worthy engines, many ground tests were performed in the months following the rollout on June 10. The full antiskid brake and air conditioning system tests, for example, were

The simple, leading-edge slat mechanism and redesigned wing-to-body fillet are part of the improvements to the 717 wing, which was based on the design and structure of the higher gross weight DC-9-34 version. To make sure the wing could handle the higher takeoff weights envisioned for the 717, the incidence angle of the entire aerofoil was increased by 1.25 degrees. Like the DC-9 wing, the 717's is swept at 24 degrees at the quarter-chord position and has a thickness/chord ratio of 11.6 percent.

completed during the run up to first flight rather than immediately after. The engine problems were finally resolved when it passed a critical full-up engine blade off test at Hucknall in the United Kingdom in July. Despite the problems, the engine also received its European certification on August 28 and FAA certification on September 1, exactly as predicted by the engine maker two years earlier.

Finally, with engine clearance obtained, the first 717-200 was ready to fly. The very next day, September 2, the assembled crowd waited in temperatures close to 100 degrees

Fahrenheit for what seemed like ages, as the 717 stood under the noonday sun waiting for a quiet spell in the surrounding air traffic pattern.

Just as it was about to take the main runway at Long Beach there was another delay caused by an inbound aircraft declaring an emergency on board. When this had finally landed, the 717 crewed by project pilot Ralph Luczak, chief engineering test pilot Tom Melody, and test conductor, Will Gibbons, lined up toward the Pacific Ocean.

Despite going to takeoff power, the engines were inaudible above even the relatively quiet TV helicopter that hovered off to one side of the airfield. After using up a considerable length of runway during its leisurely roll, the 717 finally left the ground at 12:35 p.m. Climbing to 10,000 feet over the ocean, the 717 coasted out toward Catalina Island where the crew performed tests on the main gear, engine response, flap and slats, rudder and aileron movement, speed brakes, and spoilers. The aircraft was then flown east back over the California coast and, after performing more tests and a single fly-past, landed at Boeing's test site in Yuma, Arizona, at 4:42 p.m.

Flight tests continued unabated thereafter, the crews anxious to make up for lost time and stick as close as possible to the original schedule that called for first deliveries to AirTran in mid-1999. By November, early results from the tests indicated that drag and fuel burn were "nominal or better" than predicted, leading to expectations that the baseline range and payload of the 717 could be increased. "We have been pleasantly surprised with some of the results," said 717 test and validation director, Michael Delaney. "Stalls have shown excellent characteristics and the pilots are extremely happy with the flying characteristics in general."

Vital stall tests, always a nervous time with any T-tail jetliner despite every precaution, were completed successfully after more than 200 stall maneuvers. Many were later repeated during the initial phases of the concurrent cooperative certification (C3) initiative between Boeing, the FAA, and JAA.

The newly arrived T-2 receives attention at Yuma before starting test flights. The yellowish skin of the main fuselage section, or the "elephant hide" as it was nicknamed by the test crew, indicates the parts made by Alenia of Italy. The fin was made by AIDC of Taiwan, the horizontal stabilizer was by ShinMaywa Industries of Japan, and the nose was by Korean Aerospace.

Under this pioneering scheme, the 717 was due to become the first jetliner to be authorized under a single certification basis after just one regulatory validation demonstration for both the FAA and JAA. "In the past we'd fly the FAA certification program and then the JAA. This time we will do only one with either an FAA or JAA crew member, or both," said Delaney who pointed out that the move was expected to halve the time and cost taken to certificate the aircraft.

The only problem of any significance to crop up in early tests was the discovery of an "antisymmetric squeal" at 220Hz in the antiskid/auto-brake system. These were fitted with new energy-absorbing linings to cure the problem. The spoiler system, which had been modified before first flight, was changed again after the discovery of a "spoiler float issue" that cropped up when flaps were set at 50 degrees for landing.

The second test aircraft, the T-2, joined the T-1 at Yuma on October 26 and began work principally to develop and test the advanced common flight deck systems, autoflight, and Category III autoland systems. The third aircraft, T-3, joined the fleet on December 16, 1998, and was used for assessing take-off, cruise, and landing performance. The fleet was joined in February 1999 by the first production standard aircraft, the P-1. This 717, complete with AirTran livery and a full airline interior, was destined to perform interior system and noise tests, as well as the function and reliability tests as part of the "service-ready" period with AirTran. Altogether, Boeing estimated that, barring unforeseen incidents or developments, the 717-200 flight test program would be wrapped up in mid 1999 after roughly 1,650 flight test hours.

The urgent business of selling the 717 meanwhile kicked into high gear as flight testing got underway. The slow sales had proved a constant worry to Douglas and then Boeing, mainly because it undermined confidence in the future of the program. This, in turn, tended to put airlines off the idea of buying the 717, therefore turning the sales

A close-up of T-2 on takeoff reveals the red-ringed angle-of-attack indicator below the flight deck windows and the anti-FOD (foreign object damage) deflector nestled between the two nose wheel tires. RIGHT: New energy-absorbing brake linings cured a high-pitched squeal discovered early on in the test program. The gear, made by Israel Aircraft Industries (IAI), was fitted with AlliedSignal all-steel brakes to give up to 1,150 landings per brake, or roughly double the average life of the DC-9 unit.

campaign into a "Classic catch-22" situation. On the surface, at least, Boeing maintained confidence in an eventual breakthrough. Many believed that the market would begin to show its hand as flight tests got underway, the right time of the order cycle approached, and the job of replacing older DC-9s became more urgent. Even the late appearance of the competing A318 was seen, perhaps strangely, as an encouraging sign for the future of 717 sales. As Boeing Americas vice president John Feren explained, "It creates a lot of indecision if there is a monopoly, so the presence of the A318 will create competition

The production standard flight deck of the 717, one of the most advanced developed for any commercial jetliner in the 20th century, displays its LCDs on a fall evening at Yuma. T-1 is visible outside through the flight deck windows. Note the MD-95 titles on the control columns. BELOW: The spoiler system was changed in tests after they began to "float" upward when flaps were set at 50 degrees for landing. Speed ranges varied from around 100 knots to a maximum of 400 knots achieved by T-1 early on in the test effort. The normal maximum speed was 340 knots. Changes later allowed Boeing to study even shorter field performance improvements.

and people sitting on the fence will start making decisions. We have a lead time advantage, and that's the major challenge in this marketplace."

Another factor was price. Boeing and Douglas had competed fiercely for the SAS order with knock-down prices. With continuing slow sales of the 717, the airlines and leasing companies expected to be attracted by bargain basement prices. Yet Boeing had made its offers and the list price, and though still subject to negotiation, it stood at $30.4 million. "Everybody is still looking for a bargain, but people are starting to realize that this is not a $20 million aircaft," said 717 marketing director, Rolf Selge.

Finally, new orders began arriving starting with firm orders for five from Bavaria

Flug, a German leasing company that also expressed interest in buying the T-2 and T-3 after their test role.

The biggest news came on December 9, 1998, when Trans World Airways announced orders and options for up to 100 717-200s as part of a massive re-equipment program. The puzzling news, however, was that TWA also signed a letter of intent with Airbus for 50 A318s as well as orders and options on another 100 A320 "family" aircraft.

Deliveries of the 717s were to start in 2000, with 15 aircraft, followed by 15 in 2001, 12 in 2002, and 8 in 2003. A318 deliveries were due to begin in 2003 with 11 aircraft, with deliveries continuing until 2007. The first 12 A318s, which were to be powered with the new Pratt & Whitney

The 717 was designed with easy maintenance in mind. Just visible is a mechanic crouched in the open lower half of the nacelle door, which doubles as a platform for overhaul work.

PW6000, were from International Lease Finance Company (ILFC), which had earlier that year chosen the A318 in preference to the 717. TWA said both types were ordered because of their different operating characteristics. The 717, optimized for shorter routes up to 1,300 nautical miles, was to be used mainly on shorter, high-frequency routes from the St. Louis and Kansas City hubs. The A318, with longer range, would be used on long thin routes to destinations like the U.S. West Coast. Gerald Gitner, TWA chairman and chief executive said, "The new 717s will upgrade and replace the DC-9, offering improved range and payload characteristics in state-of-the-art, environ-

mentally friendly new aircraft. TWA expects the 717-200 to deliver a 35 percent operating cost advantage over the DC-9." Alan Mulally, who took over from Ron Woodard the previous September as the new president of Boeing Commercial Airplanes said, "This decision is particularly meaningful to us because TWA looked at all its options, and ultimately they chose the 717-200 for its low operating costs and the overall value it provides."

The TWA order meant the little twinjet had at last begun to show all the hallmarks of turning into a best-selling Boeing, a curiously fitting finale to the historic Douglas line and even better news for the employees at the Long Beach Division.

The first 717-200 in AirTran colors sits in the winter sunlight at Long Beach shortly after rollout in late January 1999. The aircraft, designated P-1, was destined to partake in the crucial "service-ready" test within a few months. The following month a test 717 made the type's international debut when it appeared at the Acapulco air show in Mexico.

CHAPTER THREE

737: NEXT GENERATIONS

The remarkable story of the Boeing 737, the world's best-selling jetliner, reached new heights with the launch of the Next Generation program in 1993. Six years later, with sales of all 737s approaching 4,500, the ninth version of this sturdy twinjet workhorse was in development. Aircraft were rolling off the Renton production lines at the astonishing rate of one per working day—the highest achieved by any civil jetliner in history.

Southwest launched the Next Generation 737 into life with an order for 63 on November 17, 1993. Five years later, one of its early production aircraft is pictured landing at Boeing Field for painting after its short delivery flight from the nearby Renton final assembly line.

The Next Generation was a spectacular sales success, to the extent that meeting the demand caused a long-standing production crisis at Boeing; however, the rush to buy the Next Generation proved that Boeing had at least got the product right, even if it had seriously underestimated the challenges of manufacturing it with sufficient speed.

Like many of Boeing's best sellers, the Next Generation might never have happened. Boeing faced a huge dilemma when it faced the decision of what to do with the 737. The fortunes of the little twinjet family had improved enormously with the CFM56 engine and the other improvements that came with the development of the -300, -400, and -500 family. Sales mushroomed even as the threat from the rival Airbus A320 grew steadily.

Boeing was therefore reluctant to do anything rash. After all, what could be better than a best-selling product line for which the development is paid for and profit margins are high? It was a familiar story. Douglas had dragged its feet over developing the DC-8 because it enjoyed a massive backlog of DC-6 and DC-7 orders. Boeing, similarly, only took the painful decision to close down the 727 line after the threat of rising fuel prices and the new environmental lobby had forced its hand sufficiently to develop the 757. No company willingly takes on the massive costs of a new aircraft development if it can carry on selling its mature products.

The upgraded 737-300 and its CFM56-powered sisters were simply not as technologically advanced as the fly-by-wire (FBW) A320. Airbus, desperate to break into the lucrative North American market, presented compelling arguments to the big American operators as to why they should go with the A320 rather than the trusty 737. The arguments were convincing: a wide interior, good operating economics, sophisticated construction with advanced, lightweight composites, a

futuristic cockpit with high-tech, side stick controls, CRT-based TV displays, and a (FBW) flight control system with envelope protection.

Encouraged by favorable terms and conditions, and impressed by the new Airbus, several key U.S. airlines opted for the European jetliner over both the 737 and McDonnell Douglas MD-80/90. Northwest, United, and America West all became Airbus customers, the loss of the United contract proving particularly galling to Boeing.

In spite of the sudden campaign losses, the threat of the A320 had been growing slowly enough for Boeing to begin considering its move several years earlier. The timeline of the Next Generation 737 therefore begins as far back as 1991 when Boeing revealed that the designation 7J7, once given to an advanced technology airliner project conducted with Japan, was to be brought back to life for 737 follow-on proposals. The

name did not stick for long and, by mid-1992, the studies were renamed the 737-X.

At this early stage, much of the focus was on powerplant improvements. CFM International, which enjoyed a monopoly with its CFM56, was being threatened on all sides by International Aero Engines (IAE) and Pratt & Whitney. International Aero Engines was anxious to find a new home for the V2500, while Pratt & Whitney, itself a partner in International, was pushing a new-technology midthrust engine dubbed the RTF180. CFM International countered by discussing an improved CFM56 variant called the -3SX.

By the end of 1992, Boeing's plans were beginning to take shape as the engine issues rolled on. The airframe options were boiled down to five major proposals, ranging from all-new designs to very simple derivatives. The all-new designs were quickly ruled out because of the huge expense and the loss of

Red-painted flap fairings stand out clearly as a Southwest 737-700 soars overhead. The wing was designed for higher speeds up to Mach 0.82 and was fitted with a raked, low-drag wingtip section derived partially from the 777 design.

The most striking feature of the Next Generations' CFM56-7B engine was its 61-inch-diameter fan. Although only 1 inch larger than the -3 versions powering the 737 Classic, the chief difference was the use of 24-wide chord fan blades. These were the first ever used on any CFM56 engine and, despite being 35 percent heavier in rotor weight, brought significant performance gains.

Advanced interior architectural design techniques were developed based on lessons learned from the 777. The sculptured interior paneling and lighting helped create the impression that the cabin was larger, even though it was fundamentally identical to the original cross-section of the first 707 from the 1950s.

any commonality advantages, which were considered particularly vital in this sector of the market. The simple derivatives were eliminated early on because they simply did not go far enough toward combating the A320.

By early 1993 a group of key airlines had begun to advise Boeing on its plans and eventually chose the winner. They insisted on commonality rather than big new changes and, in some cases, voted decisively against the incorporation of high-tech features such as fly-by-wire. The recession of the early 1990s had driven home the value of reliability and dependability to the cash-strapped airlines that insisted on simplicity wherever possible.

The result was a new family of 737-X aircraft, which focused the major changes on the wing and engines to improve performance, yet retained the same fuselage, systems, and cockpit for maximum commonality with the current versions collectively renamed the 737 "Classic." The 737-X emerged as a development of the three current models with a choice of either the CFM56-3SX1 or a cropped fan IAE V2500, the -B1, as well as a much larger wing with a 24 percent larger

area. The new wing answered most of the major items on the airlines' wish list—a higher cruise speed of Mach 0.8, a bigger fuel capacity, and therefore greater range. The big wing would also allow cruise altitude to be raised to 41,000 feet.

The family consisted of a 737-300X, the -400X (a stretched version of the -400), and a -500X. On June 29, 1993, the board gave its authorization for the 737-X versions to be offered for sale and the term "Next Generation" appeared for the first time. Much to the industry's surprise, the expected choice of engines failed to materialize, CFM International having secured an exclusive deal with its new variant of the CFM56, now dubbed the -7. It later emerged that General Electric, a 50:50 partner in CFMI, had pledged funds to support the nonrecurring development costs of the Next Generation. International Aero Engines, which quickly realized it was fighting an uphill struggle given CFM International's dominance on the Classic fleet, did not contest the battle. A similar tussle was fought over the auxiliary power unit (APU), another expensive item on the air-

craft. AlliedSignal, with its newly developed 131-9(B) APU, a derivative of a unit developed for the Northrop Grumman B-2A stealth bomber, successfully secured exclusivity after tough competition from Auxiliary Power International.

On a cold, gray November 17, 1993, Boeing gave the go-ahead for the launch of the 737-X family when it received firm orders for 63 aircraft from Southwest Airlines. The airline, which exclusively flew 737s, officially ordered "737-300Xs." A few weeks later, on January 19, 1994, these were redesignated 737-700s when the deal was fully ratified and the program officially launched. The Next Generation was born.

BIGGER WINGS

The decision to go for an all-new wing, though not as dramatic as an entirely new design, was a major leap for the 737 and a first for any Boeing jetliner. "This is a first because the new 737 is the first Boeing derivative with a new wing," said Jack Gucker, the program director at the time.

The revised manufacturing processes developed for the Next Generation meant transporting fuselages in one piece to Renton from Wichita, Kansas. Until the -900 was made, the longest structure transported in a single piece was the -800 fuselage like the one pictured above. Before starting the process, Boeing and the rail company, Burlington Northern Santa Fe, conducted dry runs using a mock-up of the fuselage to ensure adequate clearance around corners, through tunnels, and beneath bridges.
LEFT: The main landing gear was lengthened and totally redesigned for the new aircraft. It was made with an integrated drag link and a one-piece outer cylinder. The drag brace and trunnion were also integrated, saving weight and complexity.

Unlike the rather stubby wing design of the first 1960s vintage model, the slender new aerofoil was reminiscent of the advanced, aft-camber wing designs developed for the 757, 767, and 777. "We settled on one aerofoil shape, one planform, and one chord, as well as sweep, dihedral, and area, when we froze the high-speed line around January 1994," said Doug Caton, who had been the leader of the wing integrated-product team. The wing was designed for flight at speeds up to Mach 0.82, though an economical cruise speed of Mach 0.79 at 41,000 feet was more likely in service, compared with Mach 0.74 and 37,000 feet for the Classic." The end of the wing was also fitted with a low drag tip, similar to the 777.

Wing area was increased to 1,345 square feet, mostly due to the increased span of 112 feet, 7 inches and an entirely new wingbox. The longer-range mission required more fuel capacity, so the rear spar was moved aft to create extra volume, resulting in a chord increase of 17 inches. The increased span also meant newly designed extended spars and redesigned fuel and surge tanks. The larger tanks held a total standard load of 6,878 gallons giving almost 1,000 nautical miles of extra range. Despite the larger wing, the designers maintained maximum commonal-

With the order book bulging, production of Next Generation 737s accelerated rapidly in 1997 and 1998; however, parts suppliers found it hard to keep pace with the growing demands of the Renton line, and at one point the line was temporarily suspended to give everyone a chance to catch up and get jobs back on schedule. These problems were largely overcome by late 1998, and production was ramped up to an incredible 24 Next Generations per month, plus 3 "Classics" per month, early in 1999. RIGHT: Fuselages arrive in the main assembly building at Renton. Some older Classic fuselages were still coming through the line in 1999 and 2000. These required joining together, while the complete Next Generation structures were "loaded" on the line in less time.

ity with the Classic fuselage by retaining the same side-of-body join location. A revised, low-drag aft wing-body composite fairing was developed to fit around the wing root.

Boeing also took advantage of the wing-box redesign to iron out nagging maintenance headaches such as fuel leaks on the traditional wing. New in-spar skins, stiffeners, and ribs were designed and produced from improved aluminum alloy used for the first time on the 777. The new design also saved weight. "All the in-spar ribs are fully machined, as opposed to being built-up. We saved literally thousands of fasteners, parts, and weight, and we also saved on the tooling," said Caton. The new tooling was designed using an improved version of the Dassault CATIA computer-aided design and manufacturing system. The tooling allowed improved manufacturing tolerances and thus cut the risk of fuel leaks.

Some weight was also unexpectedly saved in the wing as late as 1996, when more sophisticated flutter-analysis techniques became available. This showed that the wing skin thickness could be reduced aft of the engine pylon and part of the mass transferred outboard to an area near the tip. "It came out of nowhere and saved up to 80 pounds on the -800 design, around 120 pounds on the

New manufacturing and assembly processes resulted in smoother finishes for the Next Generation fuselages, as seen here on this 737-700 in an early position on the line. LEFT: The discovery of in-spar vibration within the horizontal stabilizer late in the test program had serious down-stream effects. Several aircraft already completed had to be fitted with the revised stabilizer, which incorporated a stiffening composite panel along the trailing edge spar. Here a Southwest aircraft, resembling an unfinished plastic model, is readied to receive its new stabilizers.

-700, and 200 pounds on the -600," said Caton. The skin itself was the newest type of aluminum 7055 alloy from Alcoa. As used on the 777, the alloy had high-compression resistance, which made it ideal for use on the upper wing surface, as well as for stiffeners and in-spar ribs. A recently developed 2000-series alloy, the 2324, was used for the lower skin surface which was subjected to higher tension loads.

To get more lift out of the wing, the leading edge was fitted with a new Kruger flap and an extra slat section outboard. The slat was based on a simpler design made up of fewer parts and was expected to offer better resistance to corrosion—particularly around the trailing edge wedge of the slat on the upper surface. Altogether there were now two leading edge flaps inboard of each engine and four leading edge slats outboard. Although the basic shape of the leading edge remained the same as the original, the way it was actually built was streamlined and made more efficient. "In the past, this

has almost been handmade, but now we are building it straight on to the front spar. It used to be a separate subassembly that was loaded on later," said Caton.

The trailing edge was also made simpler. The complex triple-slotted flaps of the original 1960s design, although a mini-technical triumph in its day, had also caused extra maintenance work. As one of the main goals of the program was to cut this to the bone, the new flap was a simpler, double-slotted design. The flaps were powered by a hydraulic motor that drove ball-screw actuators via a torque tube. If this failed for some reason, a back-up electrical system was designed to take over. An extra safeguard was a load-relief system that was designed to protect the flaps from excessive air loads between 30 and 40 degrees by retracting them by one position if airspeeds exceeded preset limits. Other changes to the big wing included corrosion-resistant stainless steel flap track fairings in place of the normal carbon steel. The composite ailerons at the end of the wing were also increased in length, as was the trim tab.

Another feature of the new wing that had associations with the 777 program, was the engine attachment. The new contact point between the engine pylon and wing was called the R1 fitting and replaced the conventional front and rear spar fittings on the Classic. The R1 helped Boeing eliminate a large fairing on the upper surface, therefore cutting weight and drag.

The more powerful engines also required larger tail surfaces in case one failed. The dorsal fin and vertical stabilizer were both lengthened, and the span of the horizontal stabilizer increased. The larger fixed trailing edge fin and dorsal panels were made of a lightweight, honeycomb-sandwich construction, fabricated using a glass-fiber reinforced plastic (GFRP) epoxy prepreg cured at 121 degrees Celsius. The tailcone panels were also made from a honeycomb sandwich using GFRP epoxy prepregs cured at the higher temperature of 176 degrees Celsius. Other composite parts such as the elevator, rudder, aileron, and thrust reverser were made from honeycomb sandwiches of carbon-reinforced plastic fabric epoxy prepregs.

Perhaps surprisingly, the overall amount of composites used in the Next Generation did not grow much beyond that of the Classic. In fact, some parts of the Classic that had been made from composite, reverted to harder wearing aluminum. This included areas that occasionally sustained damage of one sort or another, such as the outer engine cowl and main landing gear doors.

Renton assumed the look of something resembling a wartime aircraft production line through 1998 and early 1999 as 737 production rates rose to 27 per month, including three Classics and up to five 757s. These now included the new 757-300s, the second prototype of which can be glimpsed across the runway from this -800. Note the tail skid mounted on the open APU access panel. Both the -800 and later the even longer -900 shared this feature to offset the danger of tail scrape.

SYSTEMS TWEAKS

Reverse thrust helps slow down a Southwest 737-700 as it lands at Boeing Field after a test flight in October 1997. Boeing originally planned to deliver the first aircraft later that same month, but this was delayed until December 17, 1997, after late changes were needed to the lateral control system. BELOW: Boeing pulled out all the stops to develop this novel, upward-opening, emergency overwing escape exit to overcome a late JAA certification problem with the conventional exit. The design allowed the -600 to meet a maximum planned capacity of 149 seats, and the -800 its maximum of 189 seats. The revised door was standard from line number 26 onward and was retrofitted to some aircraft already completed.

The electrical system was one area where Boeing made a big effort to boost reliability. It was changed with "a lot of tweaks" according to aircraft systems chief engineer, Mike Redmond. "The Next Generation's electrical system is generally a lot more powerful than the -300 system and is now based on a 757-style architecture," said Redmond. Unlike the Classic system, which took power from two 50 kilovolt-ampere, variable-speed, constant-frequency generators, the new version was supplied by 90-kilovolt-ampere integrated-drive generators (IDGs). Each IDG was driven by an engine and supplied 115-volt AC power. A starter generator was also available to start up the 131-9(B) APU and act as a 90-kilovolt-ampere generator up to 32,000 feet. The 131-9 was the first APU in the world to incorporate a starter generator, thereby eliminating troublesome gears and clutches.

The new system also protected the 737 from "bus trips," which caused several problems on the Classic. A "bus trip" occurred if electrical power was lost, or disrupted. A bus-protection control unit was installed to close the bus tie-breakers to supply power from the one bus if the other failed. The unit also automatically shed nonessential loads. Each bus was protected by generator control units that guarded against differential current, over/under voltage or frequency, overcurrent, and even unbalanced phased current.

The automated electrical system control was also installed in two power distribution panels in the revamped electronic equipment (EE) bay. "On the -300 there are a lot of switching relays and circuit breakers. We've now put a lot of it down in the EE bay and out of areas where they are often more of a bother," said Redmond.

Another link to the 757 was forged with a revised fuel system that, for the first time on the 737, now included a microprocessor-based fuel quantity indicating system (FQIS). Capacitance units in each tank sent data on fuel quantity and temperature that was then used by the FQIS to calculate density. The processor then sends a fuel-weight signal via the aircraft's ARINC 429 databus (a bi-directional data highway that acts like the nervous system in a human body) to the flight deck displays and a flight management computer system. The increased size of the wing also meant more boost pumps needed to be built into the fuel tanks. In all, there were now two boost pumps each for main tank one and two and for the center tank. The center tank pumps had higher output pressure than those in the main tanks, and the engines therefore received center tank fuel first. The APU could take fuel from any tank.

Some systems, like the triple-redundant hydraulics, were "tweaked" in other ways. The hydraulics stayed the same but operated with larger pumps to provide for future growth. Engine and electric motor-driven main systems were backed up by a third standby system. This electric motor-driven pump supplied power to the rudder control

as well as secondary power to the thrust reversers and leading edge devices.

One of the other systems to be updated was the flight control, an area of intense scrutiny on the Classic following the unexplained crashes of 737s near Pittsburgh and Colorado Springs. A rash of reports of anomalous rudder movements in other 737s caused crash investigators to focus on the flight control system, and particularly the yaw-damper, as a possible contributory cause. Boeing was keen to point out, however, that the changes to the Next Generation system were more to do with improving ride quality than any suspected shortcomings. Although improvements were made to

parts of the Classic rudder controls, such as the power control unit (PCU), as a result of the investigations, the actual cause of the rudder movement that led to crashes was officially still a mystery at the time of writing.

The PCU, which moved the rudder, was made larger because the rudder itself had been increased in size. "We also took the opportunity to clean up some of the bearings and update the pressure relief valves so that, under multiple failure conditions, it didn't trap any pressure," said Peter Rumsey, who was assistant chief project engineer. The yaw damper, which moves the rudder to decrease yaw rates caused by turbulence or dutch roll, was also fitted with an electronic

The first 737-800, pictured here at Boeing Field, was the 2,906th 737 to roll out off the Renton production line. At 129 feet and 6 inches in length, it was the longest version of the twin to fly at the time when it completed a "flawless" first flight on July 31, 1997.

The squat impression created by the short fuselage, taller tail, and wider span of the -600 is emphasized in this view of the prototype taken at Boeing Field in late 1998. The aircraft, YE001, made its maiden flight from Renton on January 22, 1998.

OPPOSITE, BOTTOM: The 777-heritage of the Next Generation 737 flight deck is clearly visible with the prominent, large-format, LCD flat panel displays. The common display system could be programmed to show primary flight and navigation information in two formats: electronic flight instrument system (like Classic 737 and 757/767), or primary flight display/navigation display mode (747-400/777).

gyro in place of the former mechanical unit. "We knew the yaw damper could be improved, and most of the failures have been related to the mechanical gyro, which wears out. We also changed the electronics which go around it, which gives us better life and allows us to add [a] built-in test. So if they fail, they tell you they're failing and why," said Rumsey.

The yaw-damper system connected to the main and standby rudder PCUs, but operated independently of the rudder control system, even though it used the same actuator. It did not provide feedback to the rudder pedals but, instead, it took inertial reference inputs from its own gyro to get yaw rates and lateral acceleration. Using much more accurate and immediate data than was available to the previous system, the yaw dampers sent commands to the rudder PCUs to move the rudder and stop the dutch roll. Another change was the addition of a wheel-to-rudder interconnect system to assist with manual turns when the standby hydraulic system was on. The system sensed control wheel movements and

sent commands to the standby rudder PCU to move the rudder.

Even the air conditioning system was updated. The system used two AlliedSignal air-cycle cooling packs, a cabin temperature control system, and an air distribution system and recirculation system to produce a fresh-air rate close to 10 feet cubed per minute per passenger.

ENGINES AND DISPLAYS

Other than the radical changes to the wing, the key "game changer" to the improved performance of the Next Generation was the CFM56-7B. Designed from the outset to operate with 15 percent lower maintenance costs than the earlier versions that powered the Classic series, the –7 was also engineered to have up to 8 percent lower fuel consumption.

The main external feature of the new engine was its wide chord fan. Clearly visible at the front of the engine, the wide fan blades were the first of their type ever used on any CFM engine. The blades were made of solid titanium to maintain the

TOP: Jet Airways introduced 737-800 service to India when the airline accepted its first example in September 1998.

strength in their unusual contours and were therefore 35 percent heavier than the fan blade set of the CFM56-3 engine powering the Classic. The heavier weight of the blades meant that in the extremely unlikely event of a blade detaching from the hub, it would carry far more energy. The containment collar, which jet engines have wrapped around the spinning fan blade section, was therefore beefed up. After tests in which several more blades than expected detached, the entire collar was redesigned and stiffened again. The containment collar therefore put on unwelcome weight during the latter stages of development, as did the exhaust duct that also needed stiffening after the discovery of cracks.

The interior of the engine was completely revised and matched the core and low-pressure turbine of the CFM56-5 engine (used on the Airbus single-aisle aircraft) with a new single crystal blade, high-pressure turbine design. It also incorporated a smoother flow path and a second-generation, full-authority, digital

The large capacity of the -800, plus the extra range and low operating costs of the new version, attracted it to European charter airlines such as Transavia of the Netherlands. This aircraft was configured to carry 182 passengers in all-economy, just 7 short of the maximum.

engine control (FADEC). Even this had its problems in development, requiring new software for stall detection and recognition, after earlier algorithms failed to perform properly in all situations.

After several months of development tests in rigs and on the company's 747 testbed at Mojave, California, the new engine proved to be an excellent performer. Cruise-specific fuel consumption was discovered to be 0.6 percent better than expected. Although this does not seem a great deal to those not familiar with jet engines, it was an extremely significant result and produced a sizable margin for better range of higher payload. Similarly, the exhaust gas temperature margin was a healthy 20 degrees wider than predicted, meaning that maintenance costs would be even lower than planned. The benefit of the wide chord fan also came into play and showed that at its highest thrust rating of around 27,000 pounds, the engine had up to a 4 percent thrust margin.

There were other, equally significant changes in the flight deck, which was designed with a unique task in mind. Boeing was trying to sell the Next Generation to as many existing 737 operators as possible. Therefore, it would be a lot easier to convince them to buy the aircraft if the same crews could fly both types—current and new—without the need for expensive retraining. Yet Boeing could not afford to ignore the performance and maintenance benefits of the latest flat panel display technology. The question was, therefore, how to combine the two?

The answer was to have both. A common display system (CDS) was developed, using six Honeywell multifunction liquid crystal displays (LCDs) identical to those developed for the 777. The CDS could show the primary flight and navigation data in two optional formats: electronic flight instrument system (EFIS) or primary flight display/navigation display (PFD/ND). The EFIS format showed information that replicated that on the 757, 767, and 737 Classics, thereby satisfying existing 737 users such as Southwest. The PFD/ND format, on the other hand, looked like the newer displays found on the 747-400 and 777, therefore spreading the net wider for customer commonality.

Boeing felt sure the time was ripe to go for the newer technology cockpit, and the chance to design it into the flight deck came with a competition to supply Saudi Arabian Airlines with a new short- and medium-haul fleet. The Saudis wanted a glass cockpit with PFD format, so Boeing went to work. On paper it could not be done, but the precise detail of the CATIA system told another story. "So we just had to try it," said Captain Mike Hewett, chief pilot for the project. "It fits, but only if the panel is pushed back 15 degrees from the vertical." As it turned out, Boeing lost the contract to the McDonnell Douglas MD-90. This did not matter too much in the longer term as Boeing later bought McDonnell Douglas and ended up delivering the MD-90s as Boeing

products. The development work on the cockpit, however, more than paid off in terms of the Next Generation and later on provided the basis for a flight deck upgrade on several military-operated 707 variants such as the U.S. Navy E-6 and Air Force E-8.

STRETCHES, QCS, AND BBJS

The first 737-700 made a successful maiden flight from Renton on a cold, but bright day on February 9, 1997. Commanded by chief engineering test pilot Mike Hewett and vice president of flight operations Ken Higgins, the aircraft lifted off at 10:05 a.m. and climbed out over Lake Washington before moving to a test area over the mountains of the Olympic Peninsula.

After initial tests at 10,000 feet the aircraft climbed to 21,000 feet for basic handling checks. Top speed was restricted to 250 knots to stay within the buffet boundary.

Bright August sunshine picks out the clean lines of this brand new Continental Airlines 737-700 at Boeing Field following a customer acceptance flight. Some of the airline's Next Generation fleet were destined to be based in the western Pacific island of Guam, where they were used by Continental Micronesia to replace 727-200s.

RIGHT: Fatigue tests were conducted on a 737-800 fuselage to simulate two lifetimes of operation. To produce the effect of cabin pressure at altitude, the fuselage was sealed and then pumped up with air to 8.6 psi in less than 15 seconds during each "flight."

Next Generation and a sprinkling of Classic 737s fill the easterly predelivery ramp at Renton in mid-1998. By 2000, the site expected to roll out its 7,000th commercial jetliner—or roughly half the world's total civil jet fleet. From the 707 onward these were all rolled out of the two large final assembly buildings pictured in the top right corner by the shore of nearby Lake Washington.

Approaches to stall speed were made during which a minimum speed of 85 knots was reached with 40 degrees of flap as the stick shaker—a special device that shakes the control column to warn of impending stall—engaged. One of the most important early tests was conducted on the wheel-to-rudder interconnect system. This was intended to reduce the control force inputs when flying in manual reversionary mode (with assisted controls disabled). The new connection automatically tied in rudder movement to augment control inputs on the wheel. On the Classic, a force of almost 60 pounds was needed to turn the wheel through two-thirds of its travel in

manual backup. Boeing devised the new system for the Next Generation because smaller pilots may not have been able to handle the larger aircraft.

After 3 hours and 35 minutes, N737X landed at nearby Boeing Field where it would be based for the remainder of the flight test effort. Boeing had scheduled the flight test program to last eight months and take 1,200 hours before certification was expected in September. As it turned out, the entire certification process was a longer and more difficult affair than anyone had imagined. The failure of the telemetry system on the first flight was just a hint of the troubles to come.

Within weeks of the first flight of the -700, news emerged that new versions other than the -600 and -800 were under study. The most significant of these was the 737-900X, the ninth version of the twinjet to be developed. According to the former president of

Boeing Commercial, Ron Woodard, the -900X was a direct result of the success of the A321. "The wake-up call for me was when British Midland [a previously loyal 737 customer] bought A321s. That might not have happened if we'd had the right product," added Woodard. Another key customer was Alaska Airlines, which Boeing had already successfully wooed away from the McDonnell Douglas MD-90.

It was Alaska that finally launched the -900 in November 1997 with a $1 billion-plus order for 10 firm and 10 options. The new 900 was stretched by almost 10 feet to produce an overall length of 138 feet, 2 inches and meant that, for the first time, a member of the "Baby Boeing" series would exceed the original 707 model in length. The stretch also brought the 737 into direct head-to-head competition with the A321 which, in terms of the Airbus product line, was similar to the 757 in size. The extra

The increased 112-foot, 7-inch wingspan of the -700 and the raked, low-drag wingtips are shown to good effect in this view of a Continental aircraft on takeoff. The increased tailspan, to 47 feet, 1 inch, is also clearly noticeable from this angle.

PAGES 60–61: The leading edge of the Next Generation wing was modified with a new Krueger flap and an additional slat outboard. The wing was also fitted with a simpler double-slotted flap design in place of the triple-slotted flaps of the Classic. A load relief system was added to protect the flaps from excessive loads and automatically moved the flaps up one position if airspeed exceeded a set limit when flaps were set between 30 and 40 degrees.

room was used to seat an extra 15 passengers, enabling up to 177 to be carried in a two-class layout. Although theoretically able to handle around 200 passengers, the upper limit was still restricted by emergency exit limitations to the 189-maximum seating capacity of the -800. From an operational perspective, however, the key was that seat mile costs would be 6 percent lower.

Despite the extra size of the -900, the maximum take-off weight was still kept at the -800's limit of 174,200 pounds with a slight range penalty as a result. Nevertheless, the -900's range capability with an average payload in charter configuration was still substantial for an aircraft that had started out as a 500-mile "hopper." Boeing predicted the stretched twin would even be able to fly trans-Atlantic routes such as Boston to London, or from the eastern U.S. seaboard to Central America. Other routes included Brussels to Egypt or Saudi Arabia and Singapore to Japan.

The launch of the -900, coming as it did soon after the takeover of McDonnell Douglas, also had implications for the Long Beach production line. The -900 brought the 737 family firmly into serious conflict

Some idea of Boeing's staggering delivery ramp-up can be gathered by this aerial view of the delivery ramp at Boeing Field. In all, Boeing delivered 556 jetliners in 1998, of which 281 were 737s. By 1999, the Next Generation 737s alone were due to account for 282 deliveries with another 42 being Classics. The Next Generation deliveries were expected to begin leveling off at 275 in 2000 while the year was also due to see the last Classic handed over. RIGHT: A forlorn 737-700 destined for Russian airline Transaero awaits the completion of new financing to be approved before it can be delivered to another airline. The problems of financially strapped airlines across the world meant as many as 36 brand new Boeing jetliners were in storage pending delivery during late 1998. All but a handful were successfully placed by the end of the year.

with the MD-90, which was doomed to early closure as a result.

Other versions emerging from the seemingly endless 737 product line included a 700QC (quick change) convertible freighter and a longer range -700-ERX. Both, to some extent, used the basic advantages of the hybrid design developed for yet another derivative—the Boeing Business Jet (BBJ). This was first revealed in July 1996 as a joint venture between Boeing and General Electric, and it involved combining the 737-700 fuselage with the strengthened wings and undercarriage of the 737-800 to create a business aircraft with a range of 6,200 nautical miles.

The move was initiated by GE president Jack Welch who was looking for a new, long-range business jet. Although brand new, ultra-long-range designs such as Bombardier's Global Express and the Gulfstream V were purpose-made for the same requirement. BBJ president Borge Boeskov later said, "Jack just didn't fancy being stuck in an aluminum tube for such a long time and wanted something more spacious."

GE, through its GE Capital financial and leasing arm, was already booked to buy 82 737s, and converted two of these to become the launch customer for the BBJ. The unexpected move caught much of the industry off guard, particularly the corporate aviation community. Every type of Boeing jetliner had at some stage been either converted or

The first of 16 737-800s for launch customer Hapag Lloyd sits at Boeing Field just before delivery in December 1998. Note the upward hinging emergency exit. By early 1999, total orders for the -800 stood at more than 500. BELOW: To make space for the boom in orders and deliveries, Boeing was forced to develop new areas of the Boeing Field west ramp area adjacent to East Marginal Way and relocate some flight testing of single-aisle aircraft to Everett.

specially made-to-order for corporate, government, or private use, but Boeing had never committed to production of a dedicated biz-jet variant before.

The BBJ was not simply a 737 with fewer seats, however. It was offered with a variety of interiors ranging from luxurious airborne penthouse suites (complete with bathrooms, Jacuzzi, and bedrooms), to sophisticated office-like configurations with meeting and conference rooms as well as private suites. Some were offered as corporate shuttles seating up to 63, while another was fitted out as an airborne gymnasium for one particular owner. Other improvements were also studied to boost performance, including extra-long-range fuel tanks (fitted by a company called PATS), a higher cruise speed of Mach 0.89, and a higher maximum operating altitude of 43,000 feet. To eke out more range, and also substantially alter the external image of the BBJ, Boeing later flight tested huge, 8-foot-tall composite blended winglets designed by Seattle-based Aviation Partners. These were

initially tested on the 737-800 prototype, but after subsequent flight tests on the prototype BBJ itself, were selected as standard for the business jet.

Other corporate aircraft makers played down the BBJ gamble, but by 1999 sales had reached 50. Boeing offered the aircraft at a special offer rate of $30.5 million to entice the first few customers. This was for the "green" aircraft in its unpainted, unfinished state and did not include the extra $5 to $8 million estimated to completely furnish the jet to the typical corporate style. The price later rose beyond $32 million as more orders came in and Boeing added the Flight Dynamics Head-Up-Guidance (HGS) package and a second HF radio as standard.

As Boeing launched into the new territory of the corporate world, the 737-700QC marketers received a boost from a more familiar source, the U.S. military. The U.S. Navy was seeking a Fleet Logistics Support Aircraft as a replacement for up to 29 McDonnell Douglas C-9B support aircraft, and Boeing proposed a freighter version of the 737-700. McDonnell Douglas countered with a cargo variant of the MD-90 but was swallowed up by Boeing as the competition went on. Eventually, in September 1997, the U.S. Navy ordered a pair of 737-700s to fulfill its Navy Unique Fleet Essential Airlift Replacement Aircraft (NUFEA-RA) requirement. The $111 million contract called for delivery of the first aircraft, effectively a 737-700QC, to Naval Air Systems Command in December 2000.

While new versions were being launched and the order book began filling at a startling rate, Boeing got on with the all-important test program. A vital element of this was the recently introduced service-ready test that put the aircraft through a series of simulated airline operations to iron out any unforeseen operational problems.

The third 737-700, code named YA003, completed an intensive five-day stint of operations with Southwest on July 19, achieving 100 percent dispatch reliability. The aircraft flew 50 flights to 24 cities in the airline's network ranging from Los Angeles and Oakland to Chicago, Baltimore, and New Orleans. "Total 'flight squawks' for the 50 cycles were two burned-out light bulbs on the flight deck and a windshield wiper blade that needed a tension adjustment," said Boeing.

Just two weeks after the trial, the second member of the new family, the 737-800, made its maiden flight from Renton on July 31, 1997. Boeing test pilots Mike Hewett and Jim McRoberts reported "a flawless flight" during the 3-hour, 5-minute sortie, which ended as usual with a landing

An early production BBJ, a Bermudan-registered aircraft, arrives back at Boeing Field after its customer acceptance flight. The "green" airframes, combining the -700 fuselage and -800 wings and engines, were sent from Boeing to a company called PATS, which specialized in the fitting of long-range fuel tanks. They then flew on to one of several completion centers around the country for painting and fitting out with furnishings.

The slight gulling effect of the inboard wing section, wider tailspan, and taller main gear differentiate this Next Generation from the Classic. Note the safety cages in front of the CFM56 engine to prevent ingestion of FOD.

at Boeing Field. The first -800 was the 2,906th 737 ever built and, amazingly, the 6,508th commercial jetliner made at Renton—more than the combined civil jetliner output of Airbus and McDonnell Douglas.

TRIALS AND TRIBULATIONS

For a while it seemed nothing could go wrong with the Next Generation program. It was selling in record numbers for an aircraft that was yet to be certified, and four major versions were under development to meet market demand. Then, just as the 737-700 test team began exploring the high-speed corner of the flight envelope, the first troubles began.

During several test flights in which the aircraft was put into a high-speed dive, engineers picked up tell-tale indications of vibrations coming from within the horizontal stabilizer. The span of the tailplane had been increased by 5 feet, 5 inches over the 737-300, mainly to match the larger wingspan and maintain good pitch authority. In doing so, the aspect ratio had also increased as the chord remained essentially unchanged. Together with the higher cruise speed of the Next Generation, the combined effect on the more slender stabilizer was a barely detectable "buzz" from the in-spar ribs within the structure itself. Left untreated, this vibration had the potential to develop into something more serious.

The solution was quite simple and quickly dealt with, but the knock-on effects on Boeing's tight certification and delivery schedule were not. A composite panel was grafted on to the trailing edge spar to stiffen up the stabilizer. The vibration promptly went away, but the modification had to be cleared and it was added to the first 737-800 then in final assembly. Most of the problems affected the -700, of which several were by now either completed, in final assembly, or even in flight test.

The new 737-800, YC001, was immediately pressed into service checking out the revised stabilizer design while two of the four -700 test aircraft were working on the same task. In addition, tests had revealed niggling problems with the lateral control system that also had to be altered. If this was not enough, Boeing was suddenly confronted with a totally unexpected problem with the emergency exit design, thanks to the insistence of the European JAA.

Although Boeing had worked closely with all the certification authorities on the Next Generation, it was still taken by surprise when the European group said the exit was inadequate for new evacuation requirements. Changes were needed to enable European-registered 737-600s to seat up to 149 and to allow the -800 to seat its planned maximum of 189 passengers.

The company worked furiously at the problem, which threatened to further delay the program that by now was slipping seriously behind schedule. In traditional Boeing fashion, its engineers came up with an ingenious solution. Instead of the normal plug-type, removal overwing exit, the Next Generation was to have an upward hinging exit that stayed attached to the airframe. The door could be opened faster and more easily than the usual exit design, and by swinging up it did not impede the exit in any way.

Time was running out. Certification of the -800 was due in February, in time for the first planned delivery to German launch customer, Hapag-Lloyd, in March 1998. By this stage it had become painfully clear that the -700 was going to be well behind schedule. Certification had been planned for September 1997, with first deliveries due to start in October to Southwest. A combination of the structural changes, control system modifications, and even parts shortages from suppliers now threatened to put this back even further.

The start of November saw some better news. Within the space of a few days, the company launched the 737-900, completed assembly of the first -600, and, most important, achieved FAA certification of the -700. The four aircraft in the test effort had completed more than 1,550 flights, 2,220 hours of ground tests, and around 2,000 hours of flight testing in getting there. The first aircraft was set for delivery around November 26, but more problems were in store.

Test aircraft YA004 was prepared for a "first-of model" final acceptance flight for the FAA. The mission was usually considered a virtual formality, since certification had already been approved. To Boeing's dismay, the FAA would not clear the aircraft, citing remaining issues with the lateral control system. Flight test engineers swarmed over the aircraft, and YA002 was put into a continuous cycle of testing the adjusted flight controls. Several sorties per day were conducted with various configurations of flap settings and trim positions. Each was flown after slight adjustments to the trim system bell cranks to check for improvement.

The tests proved successful and, on December 17, just over one year after rollout and around two months later than scheduled, the first -700 was delivered to Southwest. Attention was, by now, focused on securing JAA certification that had already slipped into mid-January as a result of the exit redesign. Further last-minute changes were also required on the speed trim device, to give pilots further warning of a stall, even after the stick shaker—the long established stall warning aid that shakes the control column as airspeed decays—was triggered.

"What the JAA asked us to do was to fly beyond the stick shaker. We came close to the JAA's specific requirements, but did not meet the letter of the law which was written for older aircraft," said Next Generation 737 chief project engineer, Pete Rumsey. The advanced-wing design meant that in a stall condition "lift degrades very gradually. Nothing serious happens. There's no serious buffet and the aircraft continues to be controllable," said Rumsey. The JAA, which

Next Generation 737s returned from flight testing to be refurbished in Long Beach where they made unusual stablemates with the MD-80 and MD-90s, their once feared rivals. To cope with the massive production pressures at Renton, Boeing studied setting up a Next Generation production line at Long Beach in the half empty building used for MD-11 assembly. Long Beach was to specialize in BBJs, 700QCs, and other nonstandard versions, but the plan was later dropped. NEXT PAGE: A 737-800 bound for China Airlines of Taiwan is prepared for delivery in September 1998. A total of 65 -800s were delivered in that year.

was deliberately trying to raise the level of safety in this area, insisted on the addition of a system to enhance crew awareness. "We are adding a speed trim system that will demonstrate the stall characteristics more. It will push the nose down as the aircraft goes into a stall," he added.

The first –600, which rolled out on December 8 that year, made its first flight on January 22, 1998. The event kicked off a six-and-a-half-month certification effort that was to encompass 800 flight test hours, 459 ground test hours, and 635 flights. The number one aircraft, YE001, took off from Renton at 10:16 a.m. crewed by Mike Carriker and Ray Craig. They reported the 600 "seemed lighter and faster" than the other members of the family. Highest altitude reached during the 2-hour, 28-minute sortie was 21,000 feet and maximum speed was 250 knots. The only problem reported was a high-pitched frequency coming from an aerodynamic seal between the wing and body.

The period also marked yet another rise in intense activity at Renton which, at the end of January, saw the 3,000th 737 roll out. The same week saw Southwest announce orders for another 59 –700s, taking its total firm order commitments for the type to 129. The airline also took 42 more options for delivery between 2004 and 2006, taking total –700 orders and options to 187, of which 25 were due to be in service by the end of 1998.

The –700 finally obtained its JAA clearance on February 18, clearing the way for the first deliveries to Danish airline, Maersk. Unfortunately the very next month, one of the airline's first aircraft suffered a complete engine bearing failure on one of its CFM56-7Bs, resulting in the first known, major engine-related event for the Next Generation family. The failure forced the aircraft to divert to Sofia, Bulgaria, during a charter flight from Denmark to Crete, and it was stranded for several days awaiting a replacement engine. CFMI investigated, and, to everyone's collective relief, discovered it was a one-off incident related to a manufacturing flaw.

737 sideviews 100-200

737 sideviews 300-500

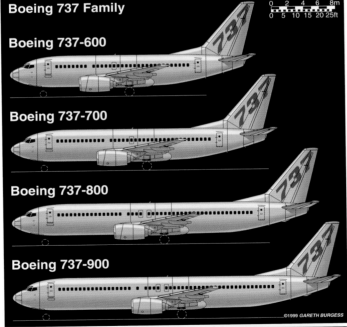

737 sideviews 600-900

BBJ sideview

Flight tests of the -600 and -800 continued at a fast pace, with the longer model receiving certification in March 1998. The -800 order book had grown substantially in the intervening months since first flight, and American and Delta were now among significant customers for the type. With most of the big issues behind them, Boeing progressed smoothly with the remainder of the -600 certification program, which was completed on schedule on August 18, 1998. A month later, the first -600 was delivered to SAS, which had launched the program in 1995 with an order for 41. By now SAS had increased its order to 55 with options on 40 more.

Only a few days before the SAS delivery, the Next Generation order book officially broke through the 1,000 barrier when KLM announced its selection of four additional aircraft, all -900s, to add to eight -800s already on order. With this order, KLM became the first European carrier to select the -900, taking total orders for the version at the time to 40. Certification of the BBJ, which had begun flight tests in August, was granted a week ahead of schedule on October 29, 1998. The hybrid version,

Major assembly of the first Boeing 737-900 was expected to begin in February 2000 with initial deliveries to launch customer Alaska Airlines beginning in April 2001. The -900 development effort was preceded by that of the 737-700C convertible by around four months.

which was certified as an enhanced 737-700, had now attracted 46 sales, though Greg Norman, the flamboyant Australian golfer who had earlier ordered one for his "Great White Shark" company, was subsequently forced to cancel his BBJ because of the Asian crisis.

By this stage, Boeing was well into a crisis of its own over production in general and the Next Generation in particular. Orders had poured in at such a rate that the company was finding it hard to meet its delivery commitments. The development problems compounded the production issues that began with suppliers down the line. After several years in postrecessionary production mode, many of the smaller suppliers simply could not speed up production as fast as Boeing wanted. Another problem was modifying and retrofitting all the early-build aircraft with fixes developed late in the certification effort.

The result was financial crisis for a program that was taking record orders. Boeing was in the process of radically modernizing its production processes, but knew that the benefits would not be felt quickly. It, therefore, took the agonizing decision of moving the break-even on the program to 400 and then 800 aircraft. It even considered opening a 737 production line at Long Beach, mainly for special configuration -700QC and BBJ aircraft, to help it meet demand. The target monthly rate by early 1999 was 24 Next Generations per month and 3 Classics.

After terrible turmoil in 1998, improved production processes slowly began to take effect and, by early 1999, production had achieved startling rates. By the end of 1998, Boeing had delivered 556 commercial jetliners of which 165 were Next Generation 737s and 116 were 737 Classics. Deliveries of Next Generation aircraft were expected to reach an astonishing 276 in 1999 and were due to peak at around 280 by the end of 2000. With production rates dropping on other types, particularly the twin-aisle 747, 767, and 777, the booming 737 line was therefore expected to account for more than half the company's entire jetliner output as it moved into 2001. The improvements in the Renton production rates meant that the Long Beach plan was dropped, though Boeing planned to use the spare capacity in southern California for 737 lap joint modification work.

With the advent of the -900, further sales of the BBJ, and the continuing popularity of the initial three members of the Next Generation family, it seemed certain that the new 737 would remain one of the company's most significant bridgeheads into the next century.

CHAPTER FOUR

747: ADVANCING THE LEGEND

April 23, 1998, was a special day at Boeing's giant Everett, Washington, site, north of Seattle. The 747-400 rolling out that morning was the 2,000th twin-aisle to be built there.

The event was largely due to Boeing's foresight 14 years earlier when the company realized the 747 needed major surgery to boost its life into the 21st century. The gamble to develop the expensive, and radically upgraded, 747-400 more than paid off. By early 1999 orders for all 747s had reached almost 1,300, of which around 570 were for the -400 model. The combined production tally for all 12 major Classic versions, including military/VIP transports, had reached 724, over 21 years of continuous production. The -400 total, on the other hand, was amassed in just over half that time.

The -400 not only rejuvenated the 747 line itself, but offered Boeing a possible bridge to the future should the market demand even larger aircraft, or should it have to compete head-on with threats from outside. All this was still way off in the future, however, when Boeing first announced preliminary details of the

Northwest Airlines took delivery of the first 747-400 on January 26, 1989—a month late due to some last-minute changes to the aircraft's state-of-the-art electronics. International services were started with the -400 between New York and Tokyo on June 1, 1989.

The famous nose of the 747 looms up on final approach. Changes to the -400's undercarriage, including new low-profile tires and carbon brakes, helped save 1,800 pounds in weight.

increased capacity. With the advanced materials and flight deck display technology now becoming available on the competing wide-bodies, and even on Boeing's own 757 and 767 twins, it soon became obvious that a significant upgrade was not only necessary but inevitable. The result was a series of five design targets for the new variant. First, the aircraft would be fitted with a raft of new technology. Second, the interior would be enhanced. Third, the range would be increased by around 1,000 nautical miles, heeding the airlines' wishes. Fourth, versions of the latest turbofans developed for the 767 and competing A310/300 models would be fitted. The more efficient engines would reduce fuel burn by an estimated 37 percent compared to the original –100 model and would, therefore, help increase range. Last, operational costs would be cut by at least 10 percent.

According to Joe Sutter, the "father" of the original 747, meeting these ambitious targets was ". . . no mean feat for a third-generation derivative based on an airframe designed nearly 20 years ago."

On the outside, the only feature that changed the appearance of the aircraft from the –300 model was large 6-foot winglets. These were based on development work originally begun by NASA Langley research engineer Dr. Richard T. Whitcomb, who had earlier achieved fame (and America's prestigious Collier Trophy) for developing the "area rule" concept for supersonic fighter design. The winglet work had taken a leaf from nature's notebook and followed the splayed wingtip feathers of a soaring bird. Aerodynamicists discovered the vortex pattern spinning off the splayed tip feathers helped distribute lift more evenly around the tip, delaying the onset of drag and promoting gliding ability. The large winglet basically replicated this phenomenon and, because it was made out of lightweight composite, created no major weight penalty. The overall effect of the winglet was a 3 percent increase in long-range cruise. It also helped take-off ability and enabled it to attain higher cruise altitudes.

"Advanced Series 300" at Farnborough in 1984. The move had been anticipated for some time. New wide-bodies from Airbus and McDonnell Douglas, the A330, A340, and MD-11, respectively, were in the works, and the latest 747 version, the –300 with a stretched upper deck, had not attracted as much interest as Boeing had hoped.

The 747-300 had provided more passenger capacity, but without any increase in range. Airlines wanted both extra range and

The winglet was mounted on a small wingtip extension, which increased overall span to 211 feet, 5 inches when empty. When the wing was fully fueled it actually bent the winglet down from its normal 29-degree angle, increasing overall span to 213 feet. The winglet, which was covered with a carbon-fiber and epoxy honeycomb sandwich, was also swept back at an angle of 60 degrees for high-speed cruise efficiency. The extra span also created room for an additional section of leading edge flap, making a total of 11 each

The massive 213-foot span of the -400 wing take the strain of a fully loaded Cathay Pacific aircraft as it leaves London Heathrow for Hong Kong. At this point the aircraft is close to its maximum takeoff weight capacity of 868,000 pounds.

A Cathay Pacific 747-400 nears the end of its journey at Hong Kong. Note the large satellite communications antenna located on the top of the fuselage aft of the hump.

side, not including the three inboard sections of Krueger flap.

The horizontal tail was also redesigned to house 3,300 gallons of fuel between the front and rear spars. This helped increase range by around 350 nautical miles. The rudder deflection was also increased by 6 degrees to plus/minus 30 degrees. This improved ground handling at high speeds and reduced minimum control speed on the runway with the rudder by another 10 knots. The 1960s technology balance weights in the upper rudder and dual tandem actuators were also replaced by three actuators with triple control valves. The lower rudder's tandem actuators were also replaced by two modern actuators with dual control valves.

The wheels, tires, and brakes, which had proved to be a heavy maintenance burden particularly on earlier Classics, were completely redesigned on the -400. The basic design of the massive, five-truck, 18-wheel nose and main undercarriage remained unaltered, but the diameter of the wheels was increased by 2 inches to 22 inches to house new, longer lasting BFGoodrich carbon

brakes. Although the size of the wheels was increased, the profile of the tires was reduced so they could fit into the same wheel well space. The new wheels were the 16th version of the 747 undercarriage, each one progressively strengthened to overcome weaknesses discovered in service. For the first time, the tire pressure could also be monitored by the crew directly from the cockpit. The redesign reduced the overall weight of the undercarriage by 1,800 pounds.

A further 6,000 pounds was saved in the wings by shifting to more advanced aluminum alloy materials. These were originally developed for the 757 and 767 and were used for the upper and lower skins of the wing torsion box. The weight benefit of this advance helped offset a weight increase in the nose area, which was beefed-up in order to correct weaknesses discovered in the Classic. The Section 41 area, which was subject to a major rebuild exercise on older 747s, was strengthened with thicker frames, skins, and doublers. It was also liberally coated with waterproof membranes, and fasteners were wet-sealed to protect against corrosion.

New engine types for the -400 included the Pratt & Whitney PW4056, which was ordered by launch customer Northwest. Derived originally from the JT9D, and known at first as the PW4256, the engine used new-technology, single-crystal, turbine blades and was controlled by a full-authority, digital engine control (FADEC). Together with other refinements, the FADEC and a larger fan gave it a 7 percent lower fuel consumption than the JT9D. General Electric was close behind, after being selected for the -400 with its CF6-80C2B1F by KLM. The CF6 was refined with the addition of an extra low-pressure compressor stage (to make four) and higher flow through the core. Like the Pratt & Whitney engine, new technology was also used in the turbine, which had directionally solidified materials in one of its two high-pressure stages. The low-pressure turbine also sported an extra (fifth) stage and, again like the PW4056, it was controlled with a FADEC.

Rolls-Royce was also offered on the -400 and gained a place for its newest RB.211-524G/H engine after winning an order from Cathay Pacific. The engine, like previous RB.211s, was a triple-shaft configured powerplant but unlike any previous 747 engine, was fitted with wide-chord fan blades. These were originally introduced on the -535E4 for the 757 and had proved both reliable and highly resistant to bird strikes. The first version was the 58,000-pound-thrust -524G, which entered service in 1989, followed in 1990 by the 60,000-pound-thrust -524H.

The other large powerplant difference between the -400 and the Classics was found in the tail. The APU was provided on an exclusive basis by Pratt & Whitney Canada, which had surprisingly beaten off competition from the dominant APU supplier, Garrett. The small APU, dubbed the PW901A, was derived from the company's trusty turboprop family and burned up to 40 percent less fuel than the APUs it succeeded—a savings worth up to $125,000 per year according to Boeing.

INTERNAL CHANGES

Although the -400 was extensively modified on the outside, the more fundamental

Boeing had to develop a modification kit for the upper deck floor structure before European aviation authorities would clear the -400 for certification. Although discovering the problem only months before the first delivery to KLM, an impasse was avoided when European legislators granted temporary certification until the development of the kit. KLM took its first aircraft, a GE CF6-80C2B1F-powered example, on schedule in May 1989.

The hallmark of the -400 was the switch to the advanced, two-crew flight deck. Improved TV-based displays, systems, and automation reduced crew workload. It also made a dramatic difference to the look of the flight deck, which had 365 switches, lights, and gauges, or roughly a third as many as the Classic 747. Here the crew of an ANA 747-400 navigates across eastern Europe en route to London. BELOW: By activating the space in the horizontal stabilizer for fuel, Boeing was able to get more nautical miles of range out of the -400. This extra mileage was particularly vital for operators on the long-haul Pacific routes such as United, which owns this aircraft seen approaching Hong Kong at the end of one such operation.

changes were made on the inside. The biggest of these was the move to a two-crew flight deck. Although the operational and technical benefits of the TV-based, advanced technology flight deck seemed obvious, questions were asked about the merit of the change because of the risk of losing commonality with existing 747s. In an attempt to resolve the issue, Boeing took the unusual step of asking the airlines themselves.

The idea worked so well, that Boeing drastically expanded this concept with the 777 program (chapter 7). The -400 consultative group included British Airways, Cathay Pacific, KLM, Lufthansa, Northwest, Qantas, and Singapore Airlines. Nearly all of them were heavily in favor of jumping to the "glass" cockpit, although Cathay Pacific originally held out for the traditional electro-mechanical layout. Boeing wanted to stick to a minimum-change philosophy to save development time and money. It even came up with a hybrid configuration that combined some of the advanced display know-how of the 757 with the current 747 autopilot.

Ultimately, however, the -400 design team gave way to the rising tide of new technology, and an all-new digitally based flight deck was adopted. The finished product was defined with the input of around 400 pilots and engineers, plus 200 nonflying technical experts, all of whom visited a specially configured simulator. The resulting display was dramatically different from the older flight deck. Thanks to the removal of the flight engineer's station, heavier reliance on automation, and a simpler systems philosophy, the uncluttered panel contained only 365 lights, gauges, and switches compared with 971 on previous configurations.

All primary flight, engine, and system information was displayed on six identical Rockwell Collins 8-inch-by-8-inch, cathode-ray tube (CRT) displays. Five of the screens dominated the main instrument panel, while the sixth was placed at the center of the pedestal between the two flight management computers (FMCs). In the event of a failure, an automatic switching system took over and display of critical flight parameters (airspeed, altitude, and heading) defaulted to standby instruments. Three electronic interface units (EIUs) together collected analog data from aircraft systems as well as digital data from communications and navigation sensors. Any one of these crucial EIUs could support independent formats simultaneously on all six displays.

The crew was shown critical data on four main displays. The electronic attitude director indicator (EADI) or primary flight display (PFD) showed airspeed, vertical speed, heading, and altitude in a TV version of the original "T" display format used on aircraft since the 1920s. Airspeed was shown on a vertical tape with pressure, altitude, and vertical speed (rate of climb) on the right. Heading was shown on a box on a compass arc at the bottom of the screen. The navigation display (ND), or electronic horizontal situation indicator (EHSI), showed where the aircraft was in space and was usually situated alongside the compass display. Novel new formats were available like an improved map mode that could project the aircraft's path for up to 640 nautical miles to give the crew an early indication

The end of another trans-Pacific flight for a Qantas -400. By 1998 the airline was among a handful using a new flight management system software package called FANS (future air navigation system). This enabled the crew to navigate the aircraft autonomously, and safely, across the vast, uncontrolled reaches of the South Pacific, saving many miles, hours, and gallons of fuel en route.

One option for extending the range of the -400 even further included using the wing box area close to the front main spar to house extra fuel. Until the -400X proposals, this area—seen clearly in this evening takeoff view—had consistently been used to store potable water.

Northrop Grumman was responsible for making all 747 fuselages from the beginning and, in concert with Boeing's manufacturing initiatives in the late 1990s, introduced an advanced fuselage assembly (AFA) process of its own. The AFA was possible thanks to newly available digital design techniques of the type first introduced on the 777, and it promised big savings in both time and money. RIGHT: Large 747 and 767 structures come together at Northrop Grumman's facility in Fort Worth, Texas. Like its related assembly site at Hawthorne, California, the Texas operation was hit by Boeing's decision to slow 747 production down to as low as one per month from 2000.

of upcoming navigation aids on an approaching coastline.

In the center of the display panel and on the pedestal in front of the throttles were two more CRTs. These showed engine and systems data in a format derived from the engine indication and crew alerting system (EICAS) originally devised for the 757 and 767. Primary engine data such as fan speed, high-pressure spool speed, exhaust temperatures, and pressures were displayed on the upper screen in either round dial or tape format. The upright upper screen, which was more eye catching, also displayed significant aircraft-status information about gear, flap, doors, tires, and fuel states. The lower screen showed secondary engine information as well as "synoptics" of the hydraulic, electrical, pneumatic, and fuel systems. This electronic page took the place of the flight engineer, and the crew could scroll through "pages" one at a time to check various systems during the flight. The "brain" of the absent flight engineer was preserved electronically in the central maintenance computer (CMC) manufactured by Collins. This was plugged into the aircraft's digital databus and, using this to

conduct interrogations, constantly monitored the health of around 70 individual systems. If it found a fault, it would identify the failed unit, alert the crew, and transmit data on the circumstances directly to ground maintenance engineers who would meet the aircraft on arrival, thus saving valuable trouble-shooting time.

The flight deck was also equipped with more advanced Honeywell FMCs that could perform calculations five times faster than the previous computers. The -400 FMCs could also perform "4D" navigation for the first time. The fourth dimension, in this case, referred to the calculation as to whether the aircraft could reach a certain altitude or way point in the prescribed time. A new autopilot flight director system (AFDS), made by Rockwell Collins, was also fitted. The FCS-700A was derived from the successful 757/767 autopilot and had a new feature called "altitude intervention" that allowed the crew to change height without having to recalculate the entire flight plan. The AFDS could also control the automatic landing of the -400 to a decision height of 0 feet with a forward view down the runway of less than 655 feet.

Giant wings dwarf Boeing workers as they are prepared for installation on the center fuselage section. Although each set weighs in at approximately 33,000 pounds, the tally could have been even higher had Boeing not designed the wings with podded engines. The weight of the engines counteracts the bending moment of the wing structure, allowing it to be substantially lighter in construction as a result.

There were also big changes in the cabin, which was refitted with a restyled interior, advanced materials, new cabin walls, and a new vacuum lavatory system. The odorless system was based on a sewer system that consisted of 2-inch-diameter waste pipes that ran through the length of the cabin. The system allowed the toilets to be plumbed into the sewer at up to 121 possible positions around the 33 "footprint" areas on the main deck and 6 similar zones on the upper deck. Waste was collected in four tanks at the rear of the belly area. Two of the tanks held 85 gallons each, while the other two each held 65 gallons. The versatile layout of the flexible interior also allowed galleys to be located in up to 12 different areas, offering a total of 157 possible locations.

The interior was lined with new heat-resistant phenolic glass or carbon composite paneling. To cut down on smoke release in the event of fire, polycarbonates were replaced by new thermoplastic composite materials. Ceilings were made from improved polyester and phenolic sheet molding materials instead of standard polyester. The interior throughout was designed to withstand heat release of up to 65 kilowatts/square meter.

Each passenger had access to much larger storage bins that were built into the side and overhead panels. The bins gave up to 2.8 cubic feet of storage volume per passenger, which was more than anything that Airbus offered, according to Boeing. The -400 roof space was also filled with a novel new crew rest cabin with bunks for eight and two seats. Another crew rest area, with two more bunks, was located on the upper deck for the use of pilots.

DELIVERIES AND DELAYS

Major assembly of the first 747-400 began on schedule in September 1987 and continued

into the winter of 1988. The aircraft was rolled out on January 26, 1988, at Everett on the same day as the first 737-400 was rolled out at Renton—the first double jetliner roll-out by the same company in history. At the time of the ceremony orders had already topped the 100 mark, and Boeing was delighted with the program's unbelievable start. Some said the -400's good fortune could not last, and unfortunately for Boeing and the airlines, they were right.

Desperate to satisfy customer demand, Boeing simply tried to do too much at the same time. It planned to begin flight tests of the Pratt & Whitney–powered aircraft in March, the GE-powered -400 in April, and the Rolls-Royce 747 in June. There was no respite in the certification effort that called for completion of flight tests, ticket award, and first deliveries in December 1988. The first examples of the CF6 and RB.211-powered -400s were supposed to be delivered by the end of the following March.

Problems began stacking up almost as soon as engineers began switching on all the complex new systems on the -400. The

A Canadian International -400, named Maxwell W. Ward after the pioneering founder of Wardair, homes in on Hong Kong. Like many Pacific-rim operators, the airline began to suffer with the collapse of the Asian economies, and redeployed its 747 fleet accordingly. BELOW: Asiana, the Seoul-based competitor to arch rival Korean Air, enjoyed double-digit growth and rushed to expand its fleet capacity with 767s and 747-400s. Like Korean Air, however, it saw business plummet in the late 1990s as the recession hit home. Here one of the airline's -400s is pictured in happier times in 1996 on departure from Seatac International.

flight deck, which ironically was designed to reduce crew workload, quickly became a nightmare of integration issues. The electrical system, for example, refused to function as advertised. It was designed with much more automation in mind, supporting automatic start-up, load transferring, and load shedding, none of which worked with anything like the 100 percent reliability needed by Boeing. Even more worrisome, particularly to the pilots, was the apparent vulnerability of the new avionics to software "crashes."

This was exacerbated by late deliveries from parts and systems suppliers, which led

Boeing to bow to the inevitable and slip the first flight from March to late April 1988. The first -400 finally made its maiden flight from Everett in April, six weeks late. The first GE-powered 747 was also late, by around four weeks, joining the test program on June 27. The silver lining to the cloud was a takeoff at the record-breaking weight of 892,450 pounds—an astonishing weight at the time and one that boosted confidence in the long-term promise of the -400.

By August, the first Rolls-Royce-powered aircraft was also in the air and the test fleet began flying virtually around the clock to try and make up for lost time. By September, the aircraft was averaging 65 hours flying time per month. Despite the effort, however, Boeing could not avoid significant delivery delays. On October 11 it admitted that "limited delivery delays" would be incurred on the first 20 aircraft, which would each be delayed by up to a month. "We intend to obtain FAA certification of the 747-400 in December, to deliver the first two aircraft that month, and to be back on our original schedule by mid-1989," said Dean Thornton, president of Boeing Commercial Airplane Group.

Even as Thornton was making the statement, further problems were cropping up on the Everett assembly line. The two most serious problems were closely related. Boeing had attempted to satisfy each individual airline by offering far more configuration options than usual. Airlines had gone mad with the flex zone arrangement and a huge range of configuration options varying from the size and location of galleys and toilets, to the color shades of warning labels on the inside of the cabin. Changing the position of a lavatory block, for example, needed up to 7,000 hours of engineering work. It was a mistake Boeing would try never to make again. The other related problem was with the workforce, many of whom were relatively inexperienced. The rapid build-up of work on the other lines, as well as the 747, had forced Boeing into a huge recruitment drive and there were simply too few experienced hands to go around. This, added to the complexity of the new -400, meant that quality control suffered and jobs were frequently turned down and had to be repeated

as a result. The issue of rework, which was to plague the Next Generation 737 line eight years later, is one of the costliest problems on any production line.

Deliveries finally began on January 26, 1989, when the first PW4056-powered 747-400 was handed over to Northwest. On May 30, SIA began using its first -400, which it nicknamed "Megatop," on daily nonstop Singapore to London services. The program looked to be running smoothly at last when, with just one week to go before the delivery of the first -400 to KLM in May, the European airworthiness authorities (JAA) said the new aircraft failed to meet new damage tolerance limits. The area of dispute was the upper-deck floor, under which ran the control cables and wiring from the cockpit. The JAA maintained the floor did not meet the latest specifications for resistance to collapse in the event of a sudden cabin decompression. Boeing was shocked, as the design was identical to the -300 and, because the loads were no different, there should be no need to meet different standards.

The basic flexibility of the 747 design enabled some carriers like ANA to operate the aircraft on short-haul, high-capacity routes and long-haul sectors. The short-haul, "D" for domestic version, was structurally beefed-up to cope with the higher cycles of inter-Japanese island travel but could be adapted quickly to long distance by adding the familiar winglets of the standard -400.

A Thai Airways International -400 approaches Los Angeles International Airport after its overnight flight from Bangkok. Note the large triple-slotted flaps and Thai insignia on the winglet.

The JAA claimed to have challenged Boeing on the issue 15 months earlier, but by delivery time it appeared Boeing had followed FAA guidelines and had not incorporated those of the JAA. The JAA, for its part, said the long life of the -400 meant aircraft would be in service to 2020 and beyond. Given that original type certification had been granted 20 years earlier, it felt it could not justify maintaining certification standards that would be 50 years old by the time retirements began. The specific reason for change, in this case, was related to resistance to bomb damage in-flight. This had not been an issue with the original design, since terrorism was relatively restricted pre-1965. Under the new rule, however, all wide-body designs had to be able to sustain a 20-foot-square hole blown in the fuselage side without sustaining floor damage that would incapacitate the control runs. The main deck of the -400 met the criteria, but the upper deck did not.

With just days to go before the scheduled delivery date to KLM, the JAA, FAA, and Boeing agreed to a compromise under which KLM would fly with a temporary 90-day operating certificate in return for assurances from Boeing that it would modify and strengthen the upper-deck floor within two

years. The deal was agreed and KLM took delivery on May 18 while retrofit kits were developed. Lufthansa took its first -400 five days later under the same conditions.

On June 8, Cathay Pacific received the first Rolls-Royce-powered aircraft, the day before the UK CAA issued its type certificate. The event marked the end of a frantic phase for Boeing, which had suffered valuable, if painful lessons. Despite the problems, Boeing achieved a remarkable turnaround to deliver all three variants within four months of each other. The main lessons included never to offer so many different configurations at once, to try to plan the production increase, to support the workforce more carefully, to harmonize certification requirements with the JAA, and crucially, to test and retest new systems before they were locked into the aircraft itself.

VARIATIONS ON A THEME

By 1993 Boeing had fully extended the new -400 family by delivering the first 747-400F. The "family planning" process began with a -400 Combi, which was completed in June 1989 for KLM. The aircraft was identical to the all-passenger model, except for a huge main deck cargo door measuring 120 inches by 134 inches on the left side. The area

around the aft section of the main deck was also strengthened and fitted with cargo-handling equipment. In normal operation, the Combi (or -400M, as classified by Boeing) could carry seating for 220 to 290 passengers and had space for 6 to 13 freight pallets. Orders for -400Ms had topped the 60 mark by 1999.

A month after delivering the first Combi, Boeing announced plans to develop a short-range version designated the -400D (for domestic use). The aircraft was strengthened to withstand the more frequent landings, takeoffs, and pressurization cycles of the short-range network for which it was designed. The aircraft was configured to hold up to 568 passengers, and by 1999 some 19 had been bought by the two major Japanese airlines for domestic intra-island services.

The fourth main version, the -400F freighter, was ordered by Air France in September 1989, spelling the end of the line for the last Classic version still in production, the -200F. The Air France aircraft was eventually taken by Cargolux, which became a stalwart supporter of the -400F. The freighter was a unique combination of old and new. It combined the short upper deck and hinged nose of the -200F with the improvements

developed for the -400. In addition, the local wing-to-body wing and fuselage strengthening designed for the -400M was further developed for the -400F. Boeing also hollowed out the space behind the upper deck to create room for two additional 10-foot-high freight pallets, making space for a total of 23. In all, the -400F had 774 cubic feet more main deck volume and up to 420 cubic feet more lower hold volume than the -200F. The aircraft could carry 124 tons of cargo over more than 4,000 nautical miles.

A KLM Asia 747-400 Combi taxies for takeoff at Hong Kong's Chep Lap Kok. Note the full left deflection of the split rudder. BELOW: Air Canada 747-400 Combi, C-GAGL, rolls out after touchdown at Vancouver International. The -400 was instrumental in Air Canada's plans to develop Vancouver as an important hub for its Asia-Pacific operations.

This intense phase of derivative development coincided with a surge in airline interest in a potential leap to a 747 successor. Carriers like British Airways, United, SIA, and other, predominantly Asian-based airlines, saw the need for a new large transport on trans-Pacific routes if the economic growth of the region continued. Boeing had studied stretching the 747 right from the earliest days of the program, but had never taken these studies further than the upper deck stretch of the -300 and -400 versions. Now, in 1991, it was asked by United to study an all-new 650-seater and, the following year, it invited a select group of airlines to discuss its early findings.

The group looked at more than 100 alternative configurations ranging from some of the original 747 stretch proposals to all-new concepts, including more outlandish flying wing designs. Overall lengths ranged from the 220-foot size of the 747 to up to 280 feet, while wingspans varied from the -400's 211-foot baseline to monsters with a 290-foot span. These larger behemoths could carry up to 750 in three classes, or almost 1,000 in single-class configurations.

By mid-1992 the group had boiled down the various studies into three major proposals. Two stretch developments were based on the 747 and a New Large Airplane (NLA) with double-deck seating for 600, a range of 8,000 nautical miles, and a circular cross-section. The airlines warmed to the NLA, but not the 747 derivatives, mainly because the former offered lower direct operating costs and higher technology. Added to this, the operators were being wooed by Airbus, which was beginning to study a jumbo jet of its own, and McDonnell Douglas,

Fresh from the paint shop, the first of five 747-400s for Saudi Arabian Airlines is prepared for delivery, which took place the next month, in December 1997. The -400 was part of a massive $7.5 billion deal, which also included 29 MD-90s, 5 MD-11s, and 23 777-200s.

which was discussing a new technology 747-replacement called the MD-12.

Boeing found itself in a strange position. It enjoyed total dominance of the market with the 747, yet could not afford to ignore the calls from its airline customers. At the same time, how could it justify the enormous expense of an NLA, which the airlines seemed to favor, over a relatively cheaper 747 derivative approach? Furthermore, how could it possibly allow its 747 customers to think it was doing nothing, while the competition appeared to be making all the big moves?

The extremely clever response to this conundrum emerged, out of the blue, at the end of 1992. Boeing decided it needed partners to make an NLA feasible. Yet McDonnell Douglas was tied up in the MD-12 and Airbus was the arch-competitor. The only aerospace companies large enough to become partners were Aerospatiale, British Aerospace, CASA, and DASA. All of them were the main partners in Airbus, yet none were actually Airbus itself. In one move, Boeing therefore appeared to sidestep McDonnell Douglas, and virtually paralyze Airbus at the same time.

Airbus management was shocked at the move, which was ratified in a joint statement issued on January 27, 1993. All the partners said they would work together on a year-long study of a project dubbed the VLCT (very large commercial transport). The study rumbled on into 1994 and, after some furious behind-the-scenes rows, even Airbus itself eventually became formally involved in the study. All the while, Boeing maintained separate studies of its own NLA and 747 derivatives, while Airbus continued studies begun in 1992 into something called the UHCA (ultra-high-capacity aircraft). By this stage the UHCA study was closer to reality, Airbus already beginning to refer to it as the A3XX.

The VLCT study finally died at a last meeting in Long Island, New York, on July 7, 1995. The study concluded that the market size was simply too small to support the setting up of a joint venture company and the estimated $12 to $15 billion cost of development. The market for an all-new aircraft with more than 600 seats, it believed, was for only about 1,000 aircraft by 2020.

747 DERIVATIVES
The death of the VLCT led to the rebirth of the 747 derivative studies, simply because

The 747 could be relatively agile when required, as demonstrated by this China Airlines -400 on finals for Hong Kong's old Kai Tak International. Note the deflection of the low-speed aileron on the outboard trailing edge of the wing.

Condensation gathers in the intakes of this Korean Air 747-400 as it accelerates into the humid Pacific air over Los Angeles International on departure from runway 24 Right.

they were affordable for such a small market, whereas an all-new aircraft was not. To keep the inertia going, and to satisfy airline demands for some action, Boeing invited more airlines to join its advisory group, which grew to include 19 members by 1995. "Eventually it became obvious that from cost and market considerations the 747-X was the winner. It was something we could afford to build and the airlines could afford to buy," said Duane Jackson, chief engineer of product development and operational infrastructure for what was emerging into a firmer program.

The idea of commonality with the 747 once more began to sound appealing to the airlines, which realized that a derivative would become available much sooner than an NLA, VLCT, or UHCA. The other spur was Airbus which, by this time, was becoming more active with the A3XX initiative. Boeing's airline group was at last giving it some definite directions to follow. The studies showed demand divided into two major camps: an aircraft with 747-400 size

capacity but around 1,000 nautical miles more range and an aircraft much larger than the -400 but with about the same range.

Boeing figured it could satisfy both sets of requirements with a double derivative. A large stretch of the -400, with a new 777-style wing and engines, would provide the answer to the high-capacity market. This version, called the 747-600X, would then provide the platform for a shorter fuselage version called the -500X. The reduced length, and therefore weight, of the -500X would ensure it had the longer range required by the ultra-long-haul sector of the market. Estimated size and performance changed seemingly daily, but overall the takeoff weight of the leviathan was established at more than 1.1 million pounds. The 279-foot-long -600X could carry 520 in a typical tri-class arrangement. The smaller -500X, at around 260 feet, was designed to carry 490 passengers across ranges up to 8,150 nautical miles. The -600X was targeted for entry-into-service in late 2000 and the -500X a year later.

With a groundswell of interest, particularly in the -600X, Boeing hoped to launch the program as early as mid-1996. A staff of engineers began preliminary design work, and a worldwide recruitment campaign got underway to populate the program. But even as the designers began work, the airlines began moving the goal posts. Most began expressing doubts over the use of current -400 technology for most of the systems. They wanted 777-style advances such as avionics, fly-by-wire, flight deck displays, and interior architecture.

Boeing wanted to stick to its minimum change philosophy for cost and time reasons, but began listening to its customers. The result was more changes by August 1996. The 747-500X/600X duo were restyled completely around 777 systems and technology, and the size and performance of both were changed once again. This time, the -600X grew even larger, while the -500X shrank. The -600X was designed with a new range of 7,750 nautical miles and capacity for 548 passengers in three classes. The -500X physically shrank by 6 feet to 249 feet in length, enabling it to fly farther with slightly fewer passengers. Range with 462 (instead of 487 as before) grew to a staggering 8,700 nautical miles. Both retained the same wing, which was unchanged at a 251 feet span.

The scene was all set for a grand launch at Farnborough that year. Malaysia Airlines and Thai Airways International signed purchase agreements for 15 aircraft between them during the weeks running up to the show, and the aerospace world waited for the other giant airlines—British Airways, Lufthansa, United, or SIA—to sign.

None of them did and five months later, on January 20, 1997, Boeing halted the entire 747-X program. There were lots of reasons why the giant 747 sister derivatives never made it, some of which were directly the fault of the airlines themselves. In insisting on the late change to 777-style systems and technology, the airlines pushed up the development price of the entire program

The astounding success of the 747, and of the -400 in particular, is exemplified by this picture of the 1,000th aircraft owned by Singapore Airlines. By 1999 orders for the 747 were close to the 1,300 mark, of which more than 560 were for -400s. The future, however, was less certain as deliveries dropped from 53 in 1998 to only 14 in 2000.

Atlas Airways surprised much of the industry and delighted Boeing by ordering 10 747-400Fs in 1997. The order boosted freighter sales to an all-time high and ensured solid production of the variant through the first years of the 21st century. Note the shortened upper deck configuration derived from the original 747-200B design.

several fold to an estimated $7 billion. This, in turn, pushed up unit price to the region of $200 million per aircraft. The resulting "sticker shock" was simply too much for any to justify, and certainly ruled out large fleet purchases of the quantity that would have given Boeing an adequate payback.

Then there was the competition, both from within and without Boeing. Within its own ranks, Boeing was successfully selling the 777 and developing newer long-range twin versions of both the 777 and 767. This was further evidence of the success of twins and the impact of "fragmentation" on the world's air transport network. The growth of big twins on point-to-point services had led to an erosion of trunk route travel, traditionally the domain of the higher capacity 747s. Boeing was worried that its own 747-500X/600X market might become a victim of the 777's success.

Airbus was also partially to blame. The European consortium accelerated its A3XX plans in response to the Boeing move and offered airlines an attractive

option with lower operating costs and promises of greater efficiency. The European design, after all, enjoyed the theoretical benefits of not being derived from a 1960s vintage design, and could take advantage of later technology.

Boeing was also busy at the time with the takeover of Rockwell's aerospace activities and, at the same time, faced the task of absorbing and digesting McDonnell Douglas. It was, therefore, a full 18 months after scrapping the 747-500X/600X projects that Boeing managed to define the next proposed growth step for the 747-400. After revisiting virtually every 747 derivative study again, Boeing came up with a relatively conservative plan to increase the -400's maximum takeoff weight to 910,000 pounds and its range to 7,700 nautical miles.

The -400X, as it was dubbed, had been outlined in previous studies as the -400IGW, but had never been defined in such detail before. It was aimed at long-haul airlines such as British Airways, Cathay Pacific, EVA Air, United, SIA, and Qantas, all of

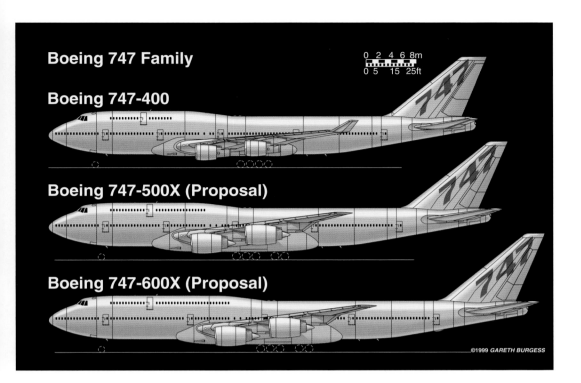

Boeing 747 Family

Boeing 747-400

Boeing 747-500X (Proposal)

Boeing 747-600X (Proposal)

©1999 GARETH BURGESS

which had 747-400 routes on which the airlines were frequently load restricted. Boeing hoped the -400X, which would be called the -400ER if launched, would solve these route problems by increasing allowable payload by at least 15,000 pounds. "Or they can use the airplane's increased range to establish new nonstop routes such as New York to Hong Kong, Los Angeles to Melbourne, or Newark to Taipei," said -400X program manager, Patricia Rhodes.

The -400X incorporated the strengthened -400F outboard wing, as well as strengthened body frames, skin, and floor beams. The gear was beefed-up with stronger inner and outer cylinders, toe fittings, steering yokes, upper and lower side strut bolts, truck beams, and axles. New, larger wheels and tires based on the 777-style 50-inch radials were also planned on the 747 for the first time. The fuselage was due to be strengthened in the section forward of the front main wing spar and part of Section 46 in the tail. Eleven frames forward of the main spar were to be strengthened,

along with the associated floor beams and skin. This was required because of the extra fuel carried on board in removable tanks, each capable of holding up to 3,180 U.S. gallons. These were to be located in the area normally used to hold potable water tanks. The water was to be moved aft to a bulk cargo area, itself requiring the strengthening of Section 46.

Boeing hoped to make a launch decision by December 1998, but with the failing economies of Asia taking a toll on Boeing's orders and deliveries earlier that year, it soon became clear that no such decision was possible. As the fate of the -400X drifted into 1999, it took with it the future direction of the 747 and all Boeing's future large aircraft plans. The -400X was crucial as a stepping stone to a family of affordable 747 derivatives, as long as the market wanted them. By late 1999 Boeing saw "light at the end of the tunnel" for the Asian crisis, and with it, the best signs yet that new 747 derivatives would follow. It seemed there was new life yet for the Queen of the Skies as it entered the 21st century.

CHAPTER FIVE

757: NEW DIRECTIONS

For 18 years the 757 shared with the 747 the unusual distinction of being the only member of the Boeing jetliner family never to be stretched. The original design, dating from 1978, had been developed as the 757-200. The shorter -100, which was aimed at the market niche eventually filled by the CFM56-powered 737-300 and -400, failed to attract any market interest and, as a result, was never built.

The 757-300 flight test program began on August 2, 1998, with a virtually flawless maiden flight. The only hiccup was the loss of the static trailing cone somewhere over the Olympic Peninsula, west of the Puget Sound area.

Minimum change was the watchword from the start for the 757-300 program. The elongated fuselage, measuring 178 feet, 7 inches in length, therefore sits on an unchanged -200 wing with a span of 124 feet, 10 inches.

The move to the stretched 757-300 version finally came in 1996 when Boeing announced the launch of the program at that year's Farnborough air show in the United Kingdom. Murmurs of a -200X long-range version and a -300X stretch derivative development had been circling for three years before that, but nothing was taken further than the preliminary design stage. The initial stretch concept (totaling 23 feet, 4 inches in additional length) was aimed mainly at providing low-cost transportation for the charter market, and in overall capacity terms, gave Boeing an effective in-house replacement for its own 767-200. Sales of the shorter-bodied twin-aisle twin had fallen off dramatically by this stage (see chapter 6), and practically the only 767-200s on the line at the time were destined for use as airborne warning and control systems (AWACS) for Japan.

Unlike previous years, when Boeing aimed at major trunk route carriers or national airlines to launch new derivatives, the changing economic conditions of the 1990s created a new emphasis on smaller, often more profitable carriers as possible launch candidates. One of these was a

German charter company, Condor Flugdienst, which already operated its packed 757-200s on holiday inclusive tour flights and was very interested in the profit potential of the longer 757. The airline wanted a low-cost alternative to its older DC-10s, which it wanted to replace on the popular "Canary conveyer" run from Germany to the Atlantic islands.

Talks became more serious throughout the first half of 1996, culminating in the launch of what was formally named the -300 in September when Condor ordered 12. The final design freeze came in mid-November 1996.

The gap between the launch of the first and second major derivatives of the 757 was therefore one of the longest in Boeing jetliner history. Conversely, the -300 development program itself was to be the shortest yet attempted by the company with only 27 months targeted between go-ahead and certification. Boeing tackled the challenge in two ways. First, it kept the stretch as simple as possible, with very few customized features for the new version. Second, an entire array of newly developed production and design initiatives were available to speed the effort, many of them inherited from the 777 and honed on the Next Generation 737 program.

DESIGN GOALS

"It is really just a fly-more-people aircraft. That's the main design goal," said Bruce Nicoletti of 757-300 product marketing. "We've increased the maximum takeoff weight capability to 270,000 pounds [from a maximum of 255,000 pounds on the -200], and increased seating capacity by 20 percent, or about 40 passengers. This aircraft will have a 3,500-nautical mile range capability with that load," he added. "The extra seating capacity, plus a staggering 48 percent increase in available cargo volume, lowers operating costs dramatically."

Direct operating costs in cents per available seat kilometer, were expected to be around 9 percent lower for the 240-seat 757-300 than those of the baseline 201-seat 757-200. More important, from the marketing perspective Boeing's figures also suggested the stretch would enjoy a 13 percent advantage over the Airbus A321-200, which had begun to make significant penetration in the market. Based on a dollars-per-kilometer percentage scale, the company also estimated the -300 would undercut the direct operating

A wide-angle view of the 757 final assembly line at Renton slightly exaggerates the longer -300 as it moves down the line alongside fellow -200s. LEFT: The stretch was achieved by adding 160 inches to the front Section 43, seen here in assembly at Renton, and the aft Section 46 which grew by 120 inches. The increased size of the section is apparent when compared to the same section for a standard 200 as seen directly behind.

Rolls-Royce took the opportunity of the -300 program to upgrade the RB.211-535E4B with a new, environmentally friendly combustor dubbed the Phase V. The -535 powered the first flight of the -300 and the original -200, making the 757 the first Boeing jetliner to use non-U.S. engines for the maiden flight of all major derivatives. Note the discolored titanium protecting the underside of the strut, the large bypass duct, and guide vanes in the exhaust in this peep up the business end of a 757-300 engine.

costs of a 232-seat 767-200 by up to 10 percent, and those of an identically configured A310-300 by as much as 19 percent. The direct operating cost difference was particularly vital for the lower-margin operations of the charter airlines, which were expected to use it mainly on routes from northern Europe to the Atlantic and Mediterranean islands.

Key to providing the magic direct operating cost difference was providing the maximum number of extra seats at minimum cost, both in terms of actual weight and development expense. Boeing eventually froze the stretch with enough room for a maximum of up to 289 passengers. This was

deemed to be the most attractive size, at the most realistic cost, and was accomplished by expanding the fuselage on either side of the center of gravity for a total stretch of 280 inches. The aft stretch was made by extending the skin of Section 46 (immediately behind the trailing edge of the wing) by 120 inches. The forward stretch was similarly produced by extending Section 43 (just ahead of the wing-to-body fairing) by another 160 inches.

"We are not adding splices, we are extending the existing fuselage section," explained 757-300 chief project engineer, Dan Mooney. By opting to stretch this way, rather than insert new barrels, the design team hoped to minimize cost and disruption on the production line, as well as take advantage of the existing design features such as the emergency exit locations. "We are going to take the overwing exit body Section [44], and combine it with a strengthened, four-door Section 46. This will allow us to meet the evacuation requirements without adding any new doors," he added.

Stretching the existing skin panels, however, produced its own set of new challenges. "Some of the fuselage panels end up as long as 400 inches. That is single panels, which present some handling challenges," said Mooney. Much of the body strengthening for the longer, thinner aircraft was incorporated in the overwing Section 44, although some thickness was added to the skins and frames in Sections 43 and 46. The horizontal stabilizer was also strengthened, as was the landing gear, which was fitted with 26-ply tires to cope with the heavier landing weights and higher touchdown speeds that were calculated as a result. Some local strengthening of the wing-to-engine pylon and strut fittings was also planned, some of it taking advantage of the recent redesign work to counter fatigue cracking that had been discovered on some earlier 757 and 767 aircraft. "The changes will incorporate this and will take account of the slightly higher strut loads that we expect," said Mooney.

Although Boeing's overall idea was to change as little as possible with the stretch, it

could not afford to ignore the march of technology over the past 18 years and took advantage of the change to introduce a wide variety of system and interior changes. One such system "bought" its way onto the stretch because of the sheer length of the twinjet. This was the retractable tail skid, which had been developed originally for the 767-300 and 777 to offset the potential for tail strikes. Even the 757-200 had suffered more than its fair share of similar incidents (mostly on landing), but this had been cured by improving crew training. Nonetheless, Boeing was concerned enough about the possibility of tail strikes that it added extra capability to the tail skid system.

The device, which was actuated to retract and blend smoothly into the fuselage during cruise, was augmented with a body-contact sensor. This was designed to alert the crew to a potentially more serious contact either on rotation or touchdown. The tail strike indicator consisted of a small, frangible foil extending down from the fuselage. If the foil made contact with the ground, then it meant the strike was more extreme than simply brushing the tail skid (itself an extremely rare event). The second the foil made contact it was designed to flash up a warning to the crew on the engine-indicating and crew-

alerting system (EICAS). In the event of an EICAS warning, the crew would have to turn back and land to complete a thorough inspection of the tail skin and surrounding area, as such an incident could have compromised the integrity of the aft-pressure bulkhead.

Another related system introduced on the -300 was a software upgrade linking the pitch-attitude sensor to the spoiler deployment system. "If the pilot is abusing the landing and coming in nose-high (above 8 degrees) and too slow, the sensors will delay

The -535 differed dramatically from the competing Pratt & Whitney PW2000 in having a triple-shaft configuration and, as seen here, wide-chord fan blades. The tall main gear, which enabled the stretch to be developed with plenty of margin, is also clearly illustrated. BELOW: The 757-300 tail skid incorporates a crushable cartridge to absorb impact damage in the event of contact with the ground. Earlier Boeing tail skids were extended by a standard oleo, meaning that the skid itself was more vulnerable to damage if the tail area hit the runway.

spoiler deployment," said Mooney. Spoilers induce a significant nose pitch moment on the 757 in landing configuration and, by modifying the spoiler control schedule for all spoilers, Boeing was expanding what it termed the touchdown protection envelope. "The action will increase the nose down force and assist the pilot in doing what he should be doing by then," said 757-300 chief project test pilot, Leon Robert. "At that angle he wouldn't even be able to see the runway over the nose."

The environmental control system was also beefed-up to cope with the larger passenger load. Air conditioning packs and generators from the 767 were added, as was a larger pre-cooler. "We are not changing the architecture at all, but we aim to maintain the equivalent flow as in the –200," said Mooney. The larger cabin was also fitted with the centrally plumbed vacuum lavatory system first introduced on the 747-400 in the late 1980s. Although this weighed more than the chemical system it replaced, Boeing hoped the difference would be more than made up by the operating cost benefits of

the new system.

The cabin itself was also extensively restyled using techniques and "new-look" materials and architecture developed for the 777 and Next Generation 737. It was given a sculptured ceiling and indirect overhead lighting, longer overhead bins and a continuous handrail which ran, MD-90 style, along the base of the bins throughout the length of the cabin.

The biggest impression, and the single most worrying aspect of the -300 from the point of view of prospective airliner customers, was the sheer number of seats in the narrow cabin. Many were worried that with a 20 percent increase in passengers, representing a typical load of 279 in charter configuration, the -300 would take too long to load and unload. Not only would this impact on turnaround time at airports, but some airlines thought it would make the aircraft unpopular with passengers and therefore holiday charter agents. Boeing took the situation seriously and measured turnaround times at Seatac Airport in Seattle. The results showed turnaround time was expected to be around 8 minutes longer for the -300 compared to a -200 with seating for 231 passengers. Total time was estimated at 66 minutes, while total time for a mixed-class aircraft with bags, but no cargo, was expected to be 59 minutes compared to 53 for the standard -200. Boeing still considered this too long and began working on ways to speed up things, such as "zonal" loading procedures such as those used by Southwest Airlines in the United States. One option was a "sliding carpet" baggage and cargo system, which combined a conveyor belt and a moveable bulkhead to provide a quickly configurable and unloadable cargo area.

Boeing also studied major updates to the flight deck, but these were rejected on cost grounds. Condor had pushed for an extensive revision based on the flat panel

Maximum takeoff weight increased by 6 percent to 270,000 pounds on the -300 compared to 255,000 pounds for the standard -200. As no extra-fuel capacity was built into the longer airframe, the overall range capability therefore decreased slightly.

Boeing 757-300

With flaps in the takeoff position, as seen in this early morning departure from Boeing Field, the slats automatically extend from the sealed to gapped, or landing position, if a stall is detected. OPPOSITE: The 14-frame, 280-inch fuselage extension is clearly evident as NU701 soars overhead on yet another test sortie in August 1998.

display technology then entering service on the 777 and earmarked for the Next Generation 737, as recalled by the airline's managing director, Dr. Dietmar Kirchner. "We would have preferred a 737 Next Generation cockpit because it would have allowed us to have thoughts of the 777 for the future. We expected more in the cockpit, but minimum change comes with minimum costs so you can't complain too much!" Some part of the –300's $65 million price tag was due to flight deck improvements, however. These included the adoption of Honeywell's Pegasus flight management system (FMS), which replaced three operations with a much more capable basic system. The FMS included the capability to operate with the FANS (Future Air Navigation System), which enabled operators to take full advantage of new communication, navigation, surveillance, and air traffic management systems under development by the late 1990s.

PRODUCTION PLANS

Boeing not only worried about speeding up loading and unloading of the new aircraft, but also how to accelerate production itself. The company faced the same problem on nearly all its lines at Everett and Renton, the most acute being the Next Generation, which faced a severe buildup rate after attracting an avalanche of orders (see chapter 3). As a result of this pressure and the need to reduce "cycle time" (the time taken from receipt of order to handover of the completed product), the company became focused on new manufacturing processes, some of which were ripe for introduction on the –300.

One of the major initiatives was known as FAIT, or fuselage assembly improvement team. This upgraded the manufacturing process used to make the fuselage, and took advantage of computerized numerical control (CNC) machines. By 1996 these were gradually replacing conventional "buildup" tools that had been in place on the Renton line since the start of the program. The old tools gradually became worn over time so that the location of positioning holes began to move. The result was increased time and money spent on rework to correct quality-control problems and delays to final assembly.

The FAIT process began when literally hundreds of original, two-dimensional Mylar drawings were scanned into digital converters. The information was then used to produce CATIA-generated three-dimensional datasets. Numerical control programmers then took this data to develop operating programs for six CNC machines installed on the line. Two of these drilled body panels, two drilled stringers (made in Korea by Samsung Aerospace), one drilled frames, and the last one was used to fabricate shear ties. With the holes now drilled precisely by the CNC machines, the fuselage parts virtually snapped together like a giant plastic model kit. This naturally rendered the aging tools obsolete, which was exactly what the Boeing bean counters wanted.

By August 1996, some 26 of the 53 skin-panel buildup tools used in the assembly of Sections 43 and 46 and the crown of 44 had been replaced by the robot machines, and the task was completed in 1997. "The big challenge has been to take the existing design,

not change it, and still end up with something flexible," said Renton 757 site-operations manager Antonio Micale, one of the key drivers behind the introduction of FAIT on the program. "We have also eliminated positions [in the factory] and combined them, so we can make big chunks of the aircraft in one area."

Manufacturing of the –300, the largest aircraft ever built at Renton, officially began on September 9, 1997, when the front left-wing spar was loaded into an automated spar assembly tool (ASAT). Jack Gucker, then vice president for 737/757 derivatives, said the event marked "the breaking of new ground for the 757," as the ASAT was akin to the FAIT initiative. The ASAT automatically drilled and installed more than 2,600 fasteners into the wing, reducing manufacturing cost and time, as well as improving quality. As with FAIT, the ASAT move was made possible by digitizing the wing design. Although the –300 and –200 wing were externally identical, the stringers, spars,

With the help of 12 spoiler panels (six on each wing), double-slotted flaps, leading-edge slats, thrust reversers, and powerful brakes, the 757-300 is brought smartly to a halt. The spoilers also provide secondary roll control in flight.

webs, and skins were thickened to take the higher loads of the longer aircraft. Nonetheless, the ASAT could accommodate both -200 and -300 wingsets.

By November 1997 the first of the huge new fuselage panels arrived at Renton from Wichita, Kansas, where the bulk of the Boeing single-aisle components are made. Final assembly of the first aircraft began in March 1998 and, right on schedule, it was rolled out under a cloudless blue sky by Lake Washington on May 31.

Despite the festivities surrounding the rollout celebrations, there was an air of concern hanging over the event. Not since the days of the 747SP had a Boeing jetliner begun life with so few firm orders, and there was little sign of new activity on the horizon. Dr. Kirchner, who was on hand to witness the rollout of his airline's aircraft, attempted to alleviate the stress. "We are so convinced this airplane will be a moneymaker for us that we've ordered another one before we've even seen it fly," he said, receiving rapturous applause from the Renton workers. With Condor's extra order, plus two taken earlier from Icelandair, the tally reached 15. A subsequent order for two more from Arkia Israeli Airlines later pushed it to 17 by the time flight tests were completed. Ron Woodard, then president of Boeing Commercial Airplane Group, remained optimistic for the long-term future of the stretch. "This aircraft is out of the ordinary and, as people recognize what outstanding economics it has, you will see

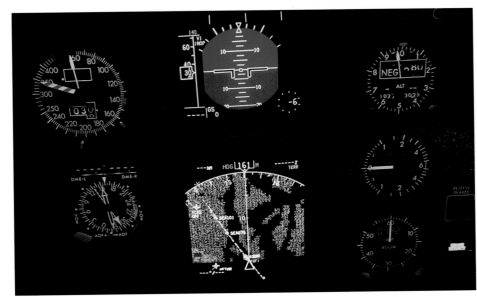

lots of them in Asia and Europe," he predicted.

But even as he was speaking, the huge production problems that had struck Boeing with such ferocity that year were about to overtake the 757-300. The planned first flight date of July 1 came and went, and still the -300 stayed firmly on the ground. Boeing blamed "production-related issues" at Renton and said the aircraft was "not the problem." The company tentatively reset its sights on July 24, but this too slipped by as the supply of critical parts to the line and the overwhelming workload on other programs took their toll on the fledgling flight test effort. Test engineers meanwhile busied themselves by fitting a landscape camera system to the belly of the -300. This option, chosen by Condor, is thought to be the first time

TOP: To protect the -300 from "abused landings," which could result on a tail scrape, the three outboard spoilers on each wing will automatically be held down if angle-of-attack exceeds 6 degrees as the aircraft nears touchdown. The resulting lift change will force the nose down, thus helping avoid an embarrassing and expensive incident. ABOVE: The -300 flight deck is virtually identical to the -200, but introduces some new features such as AlliedSignal's enhanced ground proximity warning system (EGPWS). This automatically correlates aircraft position with the location of high ground, using information stored on a digital terrain database. Any ground above preset height is overlaid on the horizontal situation indicator (HSI) as colored shading. The HSI is used for standard navigation and when the aircraft is flying at cruise altitude, the EGPWS display is dormant.

such as system had been used on a Boeing single-aisle, and it was the first application on any 757.

Finally, on August 2, the stretched 757-300 launched into the sky for the first time on a 2-hour, 25-minute maiden flight. Takeoff was made at a lower weight of around 186,400 pounds to compensate for Renton's relatively short runway. To be on the safe side, the test crew, consisting of chief project pilot Leon Robert and senior project pilot Jerry Whites, was made at a faster speed than normal. Although V1 (decision speed) was close to the -200 (at 113 knots), the rotation and climb speeds were up to 4 knots faster. Vr (rotation) was at 123 knots and V2 (climb) was 133 knots.

The aircraft, code named NU701, climbed quickly to 16,000 feet and was flown toward the Olympic Peninsula, where most of the testing was to be undertaken. Initial assessment of handling qualities with varying flap settings was performed first. All tests were made at speeds up to 250 knots, which remained the limit until flutter clear-

ance was achieved a few weeks later. Robert reported the -300 "flies very much like the -200, which is what we want, though there are some slight characteristics that might be different." The only significant hiccup during the maiden flight was the loss of the static pressure trailing cone during the first 45 minutes of the flight. The cone, which dangled free of the slipstream behind the 757's tail, disappeared somewhere over the mountains. Its loss prevented the collection of calibrated airspeed data leaving Boeing engineers to guess actual indicated airspeed within plus or minus 5 knots.

TESTING TIMES

With the month-long delay to first flight, the pressure quickly mounted on the flight test team to try to stick as closely as possible to the original schedule, which in itself was considered the most ambitious of any Boeing derivative development program. Three 757-300s were set to take part in the flight test and certification effort, originally due to be completed by mid-

December. Planners estimated completion after 725 flight hours and 1,140 ground test hours, of which more than half would be accumulated by the third aircraft in a four-day "service-ready" demonstration for Condor in November. The service-ready concept had been used to good effect on both the 777 and Next Generation 737 programs, respectively, and was also expected to prove useful to the Boeing sales force assuming the turnaround times proved as quick as predicted.

Despite the delay, Boeing still aimed to complete the bulk of the effort within the 6.5-month period originally targeted. This compared to 7.7 months for the 777-300, 10.5 months for the 737-700, and 11.5 months for the 777-200. The late first flight effectively meant sliding the entire program one month to the right. The service-ready demonstration therefore fell into December, and certification was set

back to January 1999. The knock-on effect also meant that first deliveries were delayed until early March 1999.

The workhorse of the effort remained NU701 which, by early December 1998, had already racked up 300 hours of testing. The aircraft was dived, stalled, and generally thrown around the sky to shake out every conceivable control and stability issue. As a result some changes were made to the flying surfaces and control system. These included adding vortex generators to the leading edge of the outboard flap sections to improve roll characteristics. The changes were made "mainly to give an even roll response," said Art Fanning, 757-300 chief engineer and test and aircraft validation team leader. The alterations, though desirable, were not actually required for certification and were even being considered for possible forward fit on new 757-200s.

NU721, the second test -300 nears completion at Renton prior to receiving its Condor livery. This hard-working aircraft contributed more than 300 flight test hours to the certification effort.

Changes were also made to the scheduling of the control column deflection in pitch to make the -300 "feel more like the -200 to pilots," added chief project engineer Mooney. This involved changes to the elevator feel computer and the addition of a mass balance to the column. The adjustment to the column forces smoothed out "the amount of variation that was being felt by the pilots with different loads due to the increased length, speeds, and weights of the -300," he added.

NU701 was used for some of the most dramatic parts of the test effort, including rejected takeoffs conducted at Edwards Air Force Base in California in October. The tests were made at weights up to 274,000 pounds—or almost 3,000 pounds more than the aircraft's maximum taxi weight—and speeds of up to 190 knots. The aircraft was accelerated beyond normal takeoff speed and then suddenly power was cut and the 757 was brought to a complete standstill using brakes alone. The conditions for the tests were extremely tough and not only demanded the use of brakes that were already 100 percent worn, but also that the aircraft should stand alone for five complete minutes with brakes glowing red hot before being assisted by fire and ground crews. "They seem the longest five minutes of your life," commented Mooney.

The following month, NU701 began tests with a newly installed Honeywell air data inertial reference unit (ADIRU). This new avionics unit, which incorporated air data modules made by Sextant Avionique of France, was a vital piece of the enhanced sensor suite on the -300. It was also used for the final phase of autoland trials in which the aircraft was brought in to touchdown using a completely automatic system.

The aircraft was also given the job of testing the YSM, or yaw-damper rudder ratio change stabilizer module. The YSM

NU721 lands at Boeing's Yuma test site in Arizona after another sortie. It was later to leave the baking heat of the desert to fly in search of violently strong, freezing crosswinds and tail-winds in which to test critical systems such as autoland. The search took it as far afield as Montana, Iceland, Ireland, and Scotland.

basically sensed vibration modes passing through the long, thin aircraft and automatically canceled them using the rudder. The YSM was installed to improve ride quality, but was only fitted at this relatively late stage of the effort because the test team had to make sure they thoroughly understood the behavior of the aircraft and all its various vibration modes before attempting to iron them out. The spoiler rescheduling system, installed to help avoid the problem of tail scrape, was also programmed into the YSM.

The arduous certification effort also formed the acid test for the new tail–skid actuator and Boeing's confidence that the –300 would not be excessively vulnerable to the problem of tail strike. "It has not been a significant event in flight tests and where we did have tail strikes, it's been where you'd expect them," said Mooney. Backing him up, Fanning added, "We've compressed a few cartridges [in the tail skid] and replaced them, but it hasn't been a recurring theme.

We'd laid in a supply of spares at the start of the program, which has involved several Condor pilots, not just our own test pilots, and we have not crushed any of them."

NU701 was also used for an unexpected test in December 1998 to see if up to 750 pounds of ballast tungsten weight could be removed. The weights had been added to the already strengthened wing to ensure all danger of flutter was eliminated; however, testing proved the 757–300 had a wider flutter margin than expected, so Boeing hoped to remove the weights from the production airframe.

The second test aircraft, NU721, proved an equally valuable and rugged vehicle to the test team. It built up hours at an almost unprecedented rate for any Boeing jetliner at this early development stage. "It flew through 120 hours in the first month and averaged around 110 hours in its second month and 90 hours in its third," said Fanning. "From my standpoint, that's pretty

After completing flight tests for the JAA and FAA, NU721 was sent to Hawaii where it began engine tests with the new Phase V combustor for its Rolls-Royce RB.211-535E4B powerplants.

From front to back, the marker beacon, DME and VHF antennae share more real estate than ever before on the extended belly of the -300. Note the ram air intakes for the environmental control system, which were slightly enlarged to scoop in more air for the -300's bigger cabin. BELOW: The extra-large lower cargo compartments provide a total of 2,380 cubic feet of space and can carry up to 37,600 pounds of cargo. Fire detection and suppression systems were also modified to meet new certification requirements. OPPOSITE TOP: Only 9 feet shorter than the McDonnell Douglas DC-8 "Super 60" stretch series, the 757-300 is only 2 feet shorter than the 767-300 and therefore the longest single-aisle aircraft in production in the world today.

amazing stuff. We normally consider 80 hours per month pretty aggressive."

Although many of NU721's tasks were relatively monotonous, such as long hours establishing the average fuel consumption of the Rolls-Royce RB.211-535-powered aircraft, it did have more exciting times. Highlights of NU721 tests included high- and low-speed runs through a water trough to see if the nose gear water spray deflector was necessary. Boeing had been concerned that the longer wheelbase created by the elongated forward fuselage would alter spray patterns, sending water into the engines and other inlets. The inlets and sensor ports were covered with a mixture of water-soluble paint and food dye to clearly indicate any water splashes. Much to Condor's delight, the tests showed the deflector was not needed. The German carrier had been worried that the device would be incompatible with the towbarless system installed to speed traffic on the ramp at Frankfurt, one of its main operating bases.

The most dramatic tasks undertaken by NU721, however, were the autoland tests involving landings in severe crosswinds, head winds, and tailwinds. The search for gusting crosswinds of 40 knots or more took the test

team as far afield as Iceland, Scotland, and Ireland in late October and early November. Luckily the test phase not only coincided with the onset of winter in the northern hemisphere, but also with the passage of the remnants of Hurricane Mitch over the North Atlantic. The two factors helped produce just the right conditions within a few days of one another. "I don't know who is doing the weather for us, but they're doing great and

To provide adequate exits for the -300, Boeing simply combined the "four-door" version of the -200s used by airlines such as Delta, with the "overwing-exit" version adopted by carriers such as American. The two configurations combined gave the -300 eight main door exits and four overwing exits.

Up to 279 passengers can be carried in high-density seating on the -300. Note the higher capacity overhead bins, which are 80 inches long with a volume of almost 13.7 cubic feet. The -300 also features centerline overhead storage containers for life rafts and other emergency equipment. BELOW: NU722 joined the test program later on and was used for an intensive, four-day service-ready test from Condor's base in Frankfurt. The aircraft flew on most of the airline's busiest routes to holiday destinations in the Mediterranean and Atlantic islands without a single technical hitch.

they deserve a lot of credit. We've spent a lot of time on wind watch, waiting for the right conditions to emerge, but what we've just achieved is the triple crown of flight testing," Fanning said shortly after the completion of the tests.

The third test aircraft, NU722, also performed pioneering tests in its own right when it was used for HERF (high-energy radiated field) electrical tests. These were required by both the FAA and JAA, but not when the 757-200 was originally certified. HERF attenuation tests were conducted at Glasgow, Montana, and involved checking the effect of the fuselage itself on HERF frequency and oscillation. The aircraft was also used for smoke penetration, detection, and suppression tests to check on the effects of the larger cabin and cargo compartments. Tobacco was burned to create "the right smoke" for at least one of the tests. The redesigned fire-suppression

system metered only part of the aircraft's halon gas supply into the hold if smoke was detected, rather than discharging it into the hold in a single blast. The system was also fitted with extra sensors.

NU722's biggest task, however, was not accomplished until December 7, 1998, when it made the type's official debut in Europe. Arriving at Frankfurt in full Condor livery (as was NU721), the aircraft began the intensive service-ready demonstration tour almost immediately. Over the next four days it flew 17 scheduled flights to 11 destinations across Condor's popular holiday destination network in the Canaries and Balaeric Islands. Several times the crew, consisting of Boeing and Condor staff, returned from balmy Mediterranean and temperate Atlantic conditions to freezing snow and ice in Germany.

The aircraft suffered no significant "squawks," or technical glitches, and the Condor team discovered that unloading and loading was not a major problem as had been feared. These tests were, of course, conducted only with a representative passenger complement, as the aircraft was not yet certified for commercial operation.

By the turn of the year everything seemed on track for certification, which was granted by the end of January 1999. The first airplanes were formally delivered to Condor in a ceremony in Seattle in early March, and the sales team set out to fill up the order book. A new chapter in the life of the 757 had begun.

Boeing's flight test crew crowd around the NU722 on a cold January evening in 1999, their task almost over. The aircraft had just arrived back at Boeing Field from a test sortie but virtually all other tasks were complete after 356 test flights, 912 flight test hours, and 1,286 ground hours. The 757-300 had been awarded FAA and JAA certification only hours before this image was captured.

CHAPTER SIX

767:
STRETCHING
AND
GROWING

Boeing reached a watershed when it came to the 767-400ER. It was the first wide-body airliner from any manufacturer to be stretched for a second time. It was the first Boeing commercial jetliner to directly involve input from Douglas Aircraft designers, representing a milestone in the history of U.S. civil aviation.

Boeing had been looking to change the 767, with varying degrees of enthusiasm, for several years. Most of the studies had focused on extra fuel space and revised wings to eke out more range. Together with fuselage extensions, and even curious hybrid double-deck configurations, these found their ultimate

The earliest version of the -400ER design featured a wider wingspan and winglets, as seen in this artists impression from early 1997. Aerodynamicists later perfected a revised tip design, which resembled a flattened winglet with a swept-back angle of 56.9 degrees. The 7-foot, 8-inch raked tip extended overall span to 170 feet, 4 inches.

Delta Air Lines was a big fan of the 767 with more than 80 on order or in service by early 1997 when it launched the stretched 767-400ER with firm orders for 21. One of Delta's newest 767-300s is pictured sharing the predelivery ramp at Everett with an Air New Zealand 767 and four 747-400s.

customer request for more range, Boeing knew it could do more. The problem was that doing more usually entailed extra cost, which the ERX proposal kept to a minimum. The -300ERY, on the other hand, was a far more significant change, with extra performance and higher costs.

The ERY plan involved substantial modifications to the wing to provide greater area, higher lift, lower drag, and more fuel storage capacity. The front spar was to be modified and moved forward to increase the chord. At the same time, the span was to be increased with tip extensions and winglets, while the aft fuselage Section 48 (empennage), rear pressure bulkhead, and landing gear were to be reinforced. The ERY was to have a gross weight of around 440,000 pounds, compared to 412,000 pounds offered as a maximum on the 767-300 at the time.

Boeing hoped the improved wing, complete with extra fuel capacity, would give a potential range of 7,450 nautical miles with 218 passengers in three classes. It was also aware, thanks to the 777 exercise, that airlines wanted more speed. On the long, thin routes that the 767 had largely pioneered and propagated, the need for higher cruise speeds was becoming increasingly evident the longer the routes became. The 767, which had probably done more than any other aircraft to spark the phenomenon of fragmentation (see chapter 1), was designed for a cruise speed of Mach 0.8. Airlines asked for this to be raised as high as Mach 0.84 if possible.

By 1993, Boeing estimated the ERX could be available by the end of 1996, if ordered within the year, while the first availability of the ERY would have followed a year after that. The orders did not come, however, partly because the initiative was never formalized into a firm program. To add to the uncertainty, Boeing itself confused the market by touting a shortened version of the 777, the ultra-long-range -100X. More serious still, Airbus had seen a golden opportunity and by early 1995 was well underway with a study of a proposed version of the A330, which it said "would reposition the A330 in the more active long-haul market."

expression in the 767-X of the early 1990s. This, of course, later evolved into the all-new 777 (chapter 7), but not before the baseline 767 design had been through virtually every conceivable iteration. With the focus shifting to the 777, the 767 derivative studies took a back seat for several years and reverted to relatively simple proposals for boosting the range of the -300.

By 1992, Boeing had configured two main options: the 767-300ERX and -300-ERY. Of the two, the -300ERX was definitely the easiest solution as it simply entailed adding a tail-trim tank holding 2,020 U.S. gallons of extra fuel. This would have boosted the aircraft's range to around 6,800 nautical miles and increased gross weight to 425,000 pounds. While partially meeting the recurring

The results of the Airbus studies produced various solutions dubbed the A329, the A330M10 (minus 10 fuselage frames), and ultimately the A330-200. Airbus outlined an aircraft capable of carrying 256 passengers over a range of 6,400 nautical miles with, it claimed, up to 9 percent lower direct operating costs than the 767-300ER. The consortium's supervisory board gave the go-ahead to the $450 million development program in November 1995, together with an ultra-long-range variant of the A340, the -8000.

The new A330-200 caused Boeing to take another look at its 767 plans and new urgency was injected when rumors started to circulate that Delta Air Lines was about to begin the search for a replacement for its trusty Lockheed TriStars. Airbus had begun to make impressive inroads into former Boeing territory with the A320 particularly, and the company was in no mood to let it happen again without a fight. In November 1995 at the Dubai air show, Boeing began to show its colors by announcing studies of a stretched 767-300. The derivative, dubbed the -400X, was shown with a 23-foot fuselage extension to create 15 to 20 percent more seats, 25 percent more lower deck volume, and up to 10 percent lower seat mile costs than the 767-300. At this stage, the aircraft was still closely tied to the early trijet replacement market and, with a range of 5,200 nautical miles (some 900 nautical miles less than the 767-300ER) was considered a perfect replacement for the DC-10-30.

Throughout 1996 the Delta campaign intensified, with Airbus pushing hard with its A330-200 as part of wider fleet deal, including narrow-and wide-body jets. Boeing threw its weight at the campaign and offered Delta the chance of helping to define the 767-400 as virtually a purpose-designed aircraft. Much depended on the outcome. With a victory, Airbus would secure a valuable stronghold with a new major U.S. airline, as well as effectively killing off the only direct competitor to its A330-200 variant. A victory to Boeing not only meant staving off Airbus but, more important, the launch of a

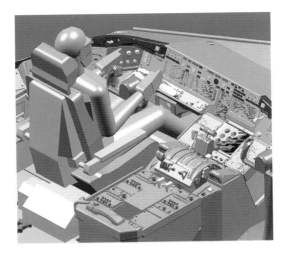

new 767 model at a critical point in the program's maturity. The origins of the 767 were traceable to 1972. It had been launched as far back as 1978. The Delta deal gave Boeing the chance to begin a whole new chapter for the 767 and extend the life of the program into the next century. To improve the chances of victory, and convinced that the -400 would find success in the market, the Boeing board authorized the provisional launch of the program in January 1997.

GO-AHEAD

With the stakes so high, it is hardly surprising that the Boeing sales team returned jubilant to Seattle in March 1997 with orders in hand from Delta. The Atlanta-based carrier placed firm orders for 21 767-400s for delivery between 2000 and 2001, as well as 24 options and 25 "rolling" options. The orders came as part of a huge fleet deal with Delta, which included Next Generation 737s, 757s, current 767s, and 777s.

By the time of the order, Boeing had already confirmed the final configuration of the -400 and was well underway with the detailed design. Six months earlier, as Boeing began working seriously on the -400 design, it realized it had big problems. Its resources were being stretched to the limit as it tackled several huge programs at once. The first three members of the Next Generation 737 family were under development, the 747-500X/600X effort was still in full swing, and the stretched 757-300 was also underway. Even the military side of the house could

Relatively late in the definition phase of the -400ER, Boeing opted to design a 777-style advanced flight deck for the new twin. The layout of the large format display system was developed using CATIA and saw the re-appearance of "Robocop"—a computerized human representation first used in the 777 program to ensure full freedom of movement in the flight deck.

The 767-400 fight deck layout was based on the large-format, 8-by-8-inch LCDs developed for the 777 as pictured here. The new layout added 21 new parts but removed 70 and provided flexibility to adapt to future air traffic control developments. Like the philosophy adopted with the Next Generation 737 flight deck, the displays could be programmed to show 747/777 style displays or the EFIS format of the existing 757 and 767 cockpits.

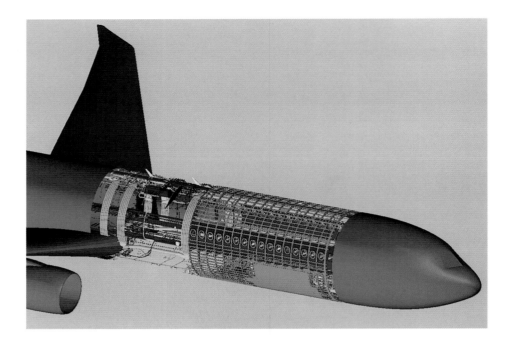

CATIA was used extensively throughout the design, which was dubbed "Stretch 2000" by Boeing. This computer-generated graphic clearly shows the 11-foot forward fuselage stretch and the ducting for the revised cabin environmental control system. About 80 percent of the -400ER was defined digitally.

By mid-1997 the final shape of the 767-400ER was being tested inside the company's Transonic Wind Tunnel in Seattle. Another model configured for low-speed analysis also completed tests that summer in the United Kingdom Defense Evaluation and Research Agency (DERA) wind tunnel facility in Farnborough, England.

offer no help as work on the Joint Strike Fighter (JSF) reached new peaks.

Boeing faced a dilemma. It could not afford to delay work on the new 767 because of the threat from Airbus, and because the market would simply not wait. On the other hand, it could search for similar skills that were being under-utilized at a famous aerospace company not too far

away. The place was Long Beach, California, and the company was McDonnell Douglas. As Boeing became desperate for skills, fate played into its hands. Just as the situation became desperate in Seattle, the McDonnell Douglas board turned down a Douglas Aircraft Company plan to develop a stretched, rewinged version of the MD-11 dubbed the MD-XX.

Ironically, of the many plans spawned by Douglas in its last few desperate years, the MD-XX was probably the best. It offered an economical, relatively low-cost replacement for the Classic 747 and the first wave of a two-generation family that offered high-capacity, long-range options to the four-jet alternatives. Despite the increasing industry unease over the future of Douglas, the MD-XX was sufficiently attractive to make American and Swissair sit up and take notice. Both reserved slots and positioned themselves to place launch orders when the McDonnell Douglas board gave it the thumbs up. The decision was

due in October 1996, and the airlines confidently predicted that the MD-XX would get the go-ahead.

The McDonnell Douglas board did not give it the go-ahead, however. Market confidence was simply too low. McDonnell Douglas' investment in the Long Beach site had been neglected over the years to the point that it would have not made economical sense to proceed. Left with no choice, and facing defeat on several major defense deals—including the JSF—McDonnell Douglas began the unthinkable and opened negotiations with Boeing over a merger.

Hank Queen, chief project engineer on the 767-400, recalled, "It was amazing. We had such a shortage of people at Boeing that, even before the merger talks began, we signed an intertechnical agreement with Douglas." The Douglas engineers, with no MD-XX to work on, were asked to help design the new features of the 767-400 empennage (including a new APU and tail skid) and wingtip areas and made up 60 percent of the original design team. As this was necessarily co-located in Seattle and Long Beach, much of the interaction between the two sets of designers was performed using real-time computer and video links. The process pioneered the "virtual teaming" concept, which later became standard practice on several subsequent programs that involved long-distance teaming arrangements.

Even as the design team drew together, it was quickly becoming apparent that the -400 was evolving into a significantly different aircraft than a mere stretch of the -300. The result was a multirole airframe that offered the potential for a growth transcontinental or a replacement for early Airbus A300 and A310s as well as older 767-200s. It was also, as originally planned, fitting in nicely to the DC-10-30 and Lockheed L-1011 TriStar 500 replacement niche.

THE DESIGN COMES TOGETHER

Though Boeing saw extensive changes were needed to meet the market requirement, it still stuck as close as it could to the simple change philosophy. Configuration objectives,

The production jigs on the 767 final assembly lines in Everett's giant building 40-23/24 area were modified to accept the longer sections of the -400ER. Here, fore and aft fuselage sections overlook horizontal and vertical tail parts. LEFT: The hydraulically actuated tail skid on the 767-300, pictured here on a UPS -300F, was modified for the longer -400ER with the addition of a crushable cartridge like that developed for the 757-300.

therefore, included not only the use of existing 767 structures, fuselage design, engine nacelles, and struts, but also the introduction of dramatically new features such as

CATIA was also used to design new assembly tools and jigs for the -400ER, which Boeing hoped would "snap together" at final body join for the first time just as the 777 had in 1994. Overall the -400ER was 21 feet longer than the -300, one of which is pictured here shortly after final body join had been completed.

a 777-style flight deck. As the same objectives also included maintaining the same type rating as the 767-200/300 and a common type rating with the 757, the original flight deck was virtually unchanged from the current models.

As the sales team notched up another success with Continental, the design team realized that tricks learned on the Next Generation 737 and 717 programs could be put to good use in the -400ER flight deck.

Part of the reasoning to go with the late change to a new flight deck was based on the availability of proven, flexible new technology. Another part was based on the simple fact that the basic cockpit had run out of growth potential as recalled by Queen. "Both Delta and Continental bought it with the existing cockpit. But, after 20 years, we've pretty much maximized what we could do," said Queen. Like everything else about a derivative program, Boeing still faced the thorny issue of what to keep and what to get rid of, and the flight deck was no different. "A lot of operators are very happy with what they've got, so we had to figure out how to develop something with commonality."

The answer came in the form of new programmable flat panel displays that could reproduce the two main forms of flight deck format used on other modern Boeing aircraft. Overall, the flight deck resembled that of the 777 with five large, 8-inch-by-8-inch LCDs arranged across the main panel. A sixth LCD was mounted on the pedestal between the two crew members. When programmed to display in the same way as the 757 and 767 cockpits, the LCDs showed flight information in an electronic flight instrument system/map format. Alternatively, if the operator wanted closer flight deck commonality with aircraft such as the Next Generation 737, 777, or 747-400, the LCDs would be programmed to show a primary flight/navigation display similar to those seen on the other aircraft types. Other flight deck changes included a new main instrument panel and glare shield, center console, and air-data/inertial reference system that integrated the air-data computer and inertial reference units.

While a lot of attention was being paid to the internal changes, the designers were also hard at work defining the external features. The most obvious of these was the longer fuselage, which at 210 feet, 4 inches, ended up being 21 feet longer than the -300ER. The stretch was made up of an 11-foot forward fuselage plug and a 10-foot stretch of the aft section. The forward plug was inserted just forward of the wing root, while the aft plug was built into the fuselage to the rear of the wing to body fairing. In a typical tri-class configuration, this longer body accommodated up to 245 passengers compared to 229 in the -300ER.

A longer body also required taller landing gear. This was important for enabling the big jet to physically tilt on the runway when landing and taking off. The existing gear would have almost been adequate, but the rotation angles would have been lower, meaning the -400ER would land and take off at higher speeds. This would mean, in turn, that it would need longer runway distances at heavy weights. "We would have had to do something anyway because we were increasing maximum takeoff weight from 410,000 pounds to 450,000 pounds," said Queen.

Boeing had to decide if it was best to squeeze a bigger gear into the same "hole" as in the current 767 or opt for a more expensive relocation. An innovative three-cylinder "shrink gear," which telescoped to allow the gear to be stowed in a smaller space, was studied. This was similar to the design used by Airbus but was dropped after airlines were worried about potential maintenance headaches. The final solution was, therefore, to move the wing-mounted trunnion 10 inches outboard and 4 inches downward, creating a bigger gear 18 inches taller than the current unit. The unit was also fitted with 777 wheels, tires, and brakes. The whole assembly was therefore larger and sturdier than previous 767 landing gears and weighed 3,000 pounds more. To cope with this weight, and to make sure the gear was pulled up quickly, a new high-capacity air drive unit was fitted. Thanks to this, payload capacity out of airports with obstacles in the vicinity was increased by 2,800 pounds.

To give the 767-400ER as much rotation angle as possible without increasing the chances of striking the tail on takeoff, a short, crushable-cartridge tail skid was designed in place of the standard tail skid. This modification alone allowed up to 1,000 pounds more payload to be carried.

The other major external distinguishing feature of the new jetliner was its unusual wingtips. Boeing realized it would need more lift from the wing if it was going to increase range and payload so dramatically, yet it also wanted to avoid the high cost of developing an all-new or even heavily modified cross-section. To handle the heavier weights, the wing was strengthened with thicker ribs and spars and increased gauge skins. The most notable difference externally was the wingtips, which were fitted with Boeing's newly patented raked extension.

The raked extension was developed to improve the overall aerodynamic efficiency of the wing and resembled a winglet that had been bent downward to lie flush with the rest of the wing. The extensions helped reduce takeoff field length, increase climb performance, and even reduce fuel burn. Traditional winglets had been considered until very late in the -400ER development, but the new device was adopted instead because the 767 wing was aerodynamically more advanced. The 767 was the first second-generation wide-body to be fitted with significantly large wingtip devices such as the raked tip and was therefore the first to be modified this way. Unlike the 747 wing, which was designed in the 1960s using principles from as far back as the 1940s and 1950s, the 767 was a far more modern aerodynamic shape with an aft-loaded, super-critical cross-section that distributed lift over a greater proportion of the surface. The wing of the 767 therefore deflected upward significantly more in flight than older wings and, as a result, reacted quite differently to the addition of a wingtip device than the 747.

The raked tips were 7 feet, 8 inches long and were made from lightweight composites with an aluminum leading-edge cuff to protect the structure. The device was canted back sharply at an angle of 56.9 degrees and was supported on the wingtip by an aluminum spar. Wing aspect ratio increased from 7.99 to 9.27 as a result of the changes, leading to expectations that cruise performance would be enhanced significantly. Other than a change to the outermost leading edge slat, the basic wing needed no

Although some parts changed out of all recognition, the overall cost of the -400ER effort was kept down by retaining commonality wherever possible. The large horizontal stabilizers for example, one of which is seen here under construction at Northrop Grumman's Fort Worth site in Texas, remained essentially identical apart from the localized strengthening for higher loads.

The launch engine for the 767-400ER was General Electric's CF6-80C2B7F1, one of which is seen awaiting test runs at the company's Peebles test site in Ohio in January 1999. The engine was rated at 62,100 pounds of thrust, but was scheduled to grow quickly as the B8F version to 63,500 pounds and beyond. The engine was the first to incorporate the newly developed "boltless" turbine technology, which improved performance and reduced weight and parts count.

The economy section of the "new look" 767-400ER interior was mocked-up for viewing by potential airline customers. The interior featured the sculpted ceiling, panels, and indirect lighting of the 777 and new storage bins, which provided each passenger with a more than 10 percent increase in storage volume. The cross-sectional area of the center bins, for example, was increased to 282 square inches, or 16 percent more than the -300 bin. The -400ER could carry between 245 passengers in a three-class configuration and up to 375 in all-economy.

major changes to support the tip, and the design was such that if either wingtip was somehow damaged in an incident, the -400ER could be dispatched on another flight with both removed.

Another advantage was improved access to airport gates. "The baseline configuration had a span of 181 feet with winglets, which was chosen before we really began the wingtip studies," said Queen. The slightly smaller span achieved with the raked tips therefore not only allowed Boeing to meet the long-range mission goals, but also to use the same gates as the DC-10 and L-1011.

POWERFUL ADVANCES

One of the other major attractions of the -400ER was that existing 767 engines could be used to power the new derivative. This not only reduced development costs, but made certification an easier and speedier prospect. General Electric and Pratt & Whitney, the dominant suppliers to the 767 program, needed only to make relatively minor adaptations to the CF6-80C2 and PW4000, respectively. These included changes to the external accessories around the engine to help feed power to the -400ER's 120 kilovolt-ampere electrical system. This was based around integrated-

drive generators (IDGs), the type adopted for the 777, and provided benefits such as no-break power transfers, minimizing potentially damaging power supply interruptions to on-board systems.

The two GE offerings were the 62,100-pound thrust CF6-80C2B7F1 engine, or the slightly more powerful B8F1 rated at 63,500 pounds of thrust. Both used the company's recently developed "boltless" turbine technology and provided GE with a possible growth path to a more powerful 67,500-pound thrust class engine. This proved an attractive target to both GE and Boeing for several reasons. To GE it was a good reason to grow its reliable CF6, without great risk, to meet the power demands of an even more capable heavy-weight 767-400ER and proposed growth versions of the 747-400 at the same time (see chapter 4). To Boeing, it enabled the design team to study a 767-400 version with 10,000 pounds of extra weight. This was mostly made up of fuel stored in the horizontal tail, and extended the aircraft's range well beyond the current -400ER maximum. The extra availability on the 747 growth versions was an added bonus.

Pratt & Whitney similarly was anxious to use the 767-400ER as a step up to the potential opportunity offered by the 747

growth studies. Although GE and Pratt & Whitney had teamed in 1996 to form the Engine Alliance, the two focused their efforts on the GP7000 engine for the Airbus A3XX, rather than the 747 following Boeing's decision to abandon the 747-500X and 747-600X derivatives. It was, therefore, back to the familiar open competition between the two as Pratt & Whitney worked on modifying the PW4062 for the new 767.

Rolls-Royce considered opting out of the 767-400 race early on. The company had never really enjoyed its relationship with the 767, which had been aimed specifically at fitting the RB.211-524H for the British Airways fleet. With the exception of an isolated sale to the Chinese, the RB.211-524 option on the 767 never really took off. Later operational problems on the -524H in service with the 767 later prompted Rolls-Royce into developing the -524G/T hybrid. This engine, which combined elements of the Trent 800 core with the -524G/H, became the standard offering on both the 747-400 and 767-300. In addition to its poor market position on the 767, Rolls-Royce could not meet the higher thrust requirement of the -400ER without switching to a larger fan in order to meet Stage 3 noise requirements. It nevertheless began studies of a rebladed version of the Trent 500, designated the Trent 600.

Another, often overlooked, engine was also selected for the 767-400ER. The higher power and air-conditioning requirements of the larger cabin drove the development of a new tail-mounted APU. AlliedSignal, which supplied the bulk of APUs for the Airbus and Boeing products, developed the 331-400, which was 40 percent more powerful than the GTCP332 found on current -300s.

The bigger cabin for which the APU was designed was to be serviced with bigger water and waste capacity. The amount of potable water was increased by 75 gallons and the capacity of the waste system was boosted by 30 gallons.

The larger water and waste tanks were located in the bulk cargo compartment and reduced its area to 345 cubic feet from 430

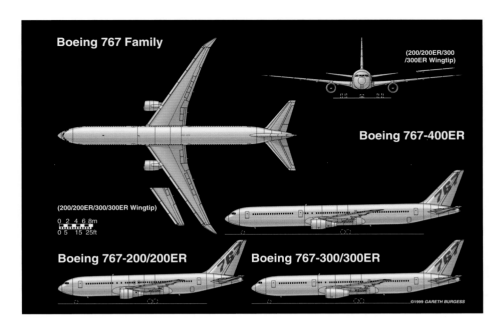

cubic feet on the 767-300. This was more than offset by the bigger forward and aft cargo compartments, however. In all, the -400ER could carry one extra 96-by-125-inch pallet and four extra LD-2 containers, providing an extra 810 cubic feet of cargo capacity. More changes were also introduced on the passenger deck, which was outfitted with an interior based heavily on that of the 777. Key to the changes was a streamlined interior architecture and pivot-type stow bins that, on the outboard stations, could each accommodate two roll-on bags stowed crossways. The high-tech interior was completed with ceiling-mounted, retractable LCD monitors. Longer escape slides were also added to doors 1, 2, and 3 because of the longer drop to the ground that would result from a nose or main gear collapse.

Construction of the first part of the -400ER began in July 1998 when the initial set of landing gear forgings were cast. At roughly the same time, the first wing-rib posts were being built at Boeing's Auburn site in Washington. All the parts began to come together on schedule for final body join at Everett in June 1999. Rollout took place at the end of August and the first flight was tentatively on track for early October 1999. The 767-400 was set for a fast-paced certification effort, and first deliveries to Delta were scheduled for May 2000.

Side by side comparisons of 767-200/300 and -400

CHAPTER SEVEN

777: THE MAGNIFICENT SEVENTH

Boeing's seventh major jetliner model, the 777, was the company's single most important development since the 747. The 777 generated changes throughout Boeing in every direction, from technical advancement to corporate strategy.

Technically, it was not only the world's largest and fastest twinjet, but used the most powerful jet engines ever built. Strategically the 777 changed not only the way Boeing developed civil and military aircraft, but it set in motion a chain of events that altered the company's entire manufacturing and marketing outlook. Crucially it also provided fertile ground for new market expansion at the expense of McDonnell Douglas and, more important, Airbus Industrie.

British Airways became directly involved in the design of the 777 from the start of the program and suggested more than 100 changes to the aircraft, including many aspects of the interior. Here, G-ZZZB nears Boeing Field on completion of another predelivery test flight.

Other than perhaps the last point, none of these far-reaching effects were foreseen in 1986 when the 777 story really began. Urged on by its own forecast people, Boeing began to look at ways of replacing the large fleets of McDonnell Douglas DC-10s and Lockheed L-1011 TriStars that would be retiring in the 1990s. Boeing believed the simplest way to attack this potentially huge market was with a stretched derivative of the 767-300, which could be sized to offer the same capacity as the older trijets.

It is at this point, however, that the 777 story begins to diverge from the traditional path established so clearly with its predecessors. The airlines did not react well to Boeing's early proposals, which were loosely dubbed the 767-X. The operators of the late 1980s were becoming more sophisticated, and their requirements for larger aircraft were becoming more specific. Additionally, the competition was stepping up to a fierce new level with both Airbus and McDonnell Douglas offering new products in roughly the same market segment. Airbus was working on the A330 and A340, a set of sister wide-body aircraft for medium- and long-haul routes, while McDonnell Douglas was developing the MD-11, a radically revised and stretched derivative of the DC-10.

The combined effect of these factors had a profound influence on Boeing which, by 1988, realized that something larger than a 767 derivative was going to be needed. To find out exactly what would meet the requirement, Boeing turned the problem on

United's N777UA waits to cross the active runway at Los Angeles International Airport. United's DC-10 replacement initiative provided the impetus for the launch of the 777 program in October 1991.

its head and decided to make the 767-X a "market-driven" project. From this point on, the airlines themselves were asked to become members of the design team. They would be essentially advising the company on the new design every step of the way.

The project received further stimulus that year when United Airlines began its own search for a DC-10 replacement. The "Diesel Ten" fleet replacement study, as it was nicknamed, dovetailed well with Boeing's own 767-X initiative, but provided Boeing with a specific requirement at which to aim its efforts. With the inertia building by late 1989, the pressure was on to try to firm up its plans. On December 8, 1989, the Boeing board authorized the Commercial Airplane Group to begin issuing firm offers to airlines on the 767-X. Boeing decided it was definitely going to be in the DC-10 replacement business, now all it needed to do was figure out exactly what it was going to build.

At this late stage the influence of the 767 could still be seen on the evolving design, despite the growing dimensions on all sides.

The fuselage cross-section had grown to 19 feet, 11 inches, 41 inches wider and 16 feet longer than the 767-300. The new wing also made its first appearance with a span of 170 feet, or 14 feet wider than the 767, with the addition of winglets. The 767-X was also expected to retain the existing 767 flight deck, nose and afterbody, including nose undercarriage and wheel well. The aircraft was designed to retain the 767 vertical tail and empennage but with a modified Section 48 and a 52.4-inch root insert on the horizontal stabilizer.

WORKING TOGETHER

The dramatic effect of the airlines on the 767-X design began to be felt in January 1990, when Boeing invited technical representatives from eight leading world airlines to sit around the table for a "working together" meeting. The members of the "gang of eight," as it was called, included All Nippon Airways (ANA), American Airlines, British Airways, Cathay Pacific, Delta Air Lines, Japan Air Lines, Qantas, and United Airlines. All were asked to fill out a 23-page

Thanks largely to the input of Cathay Pacific, the fuselage width of the 777 grew from that of the 767 to 747-like proportions. The airline's first 777, and the first Rolls-Royce–powered aircraft, is pictured during the ETOPS test phase of the certification program in July 1995.

All Nippon Airways was a member of the original "working together" team and recommended the baseline -200 be stretched by several frames. The APU inlet is deployed in the open position on this ANA aircraft seen here taxing at Tokyo's Haneda airport in Japan.

questionnaire, and the results were startling. Even the revised "maximum change" 767-X was totally unacceptable to the gang.

Boeing chairman and CEO Philip Condit was the first leader of the newly created 777 Division of Boeing Commercial Airplane Group. He recalled the innovative approach: "In designing the new 777, we established a new way of working at Boeing, adopting methods which proved so effective they are being incorporated into programs across the company. For want of a more original phrase, we called this concept 'working together'.

"Nobody is as smart as all of us," Condit added. "In other words, we airplane designers are very smart, but we become even smarter when we listen to people who are not airplane designers—people like customers and suppliers and professionals from other disciplines within our own company."

The new team quickly moved into action and, by March 1990, produced a basic configuration for a new-look 767-X. At the

insistence of Cathay Pacific, the fuselage diameter was enlarged to within a few inches of the 747. This allowed up to 325 passengers to be carried in a tri-class arrangement and suited the needs of all the Asian carriers in particular. ANA asked for the baseline model to be stretched slightly to add a few more seat rows while airlines like United pressed for advanced flight deck and flight control systems. Others such as British Airways pushed for highly flexible interiors, a high degree of built-in tests, and a target of 10 percent better dollars-per-aircraft-seat-mile cost than either the A330 or MD-11. American asked for gate commonality with the DC-10, while United urged Boeing to develop the 767-X with "instant ETOPS" (extended range twin operations) from the first day in service. In the past, any twinjet venturing over unusually long, oceanic distances had to earn the right to fly up to three hours away from a suitable diversionary airport by operating for thousands of trouble-free hours in service.

An Emirates 777 crew gives Iraq a wide berth as they pass to the south of the no-fly zone en route from Dubai to London. The 777 flight deck combined an advanced version of the 747 display concept with the twinjet systems philosophy of the 767. BELOW: The heart and brain of the 777 is here, in the electronic equipment bay below the flight deck. The core of the entire system, however, is the Honeywell-developed Aircraft Information Management System (AIMS), which has yet to be installed in the packed racks.

The reference to ETOPS at this early stage also indicated that everyone was by now firmly convinced the aircraft would have two engines, rather than three or even four. The twin configuration had become popular with Boeing from the 737 onward, but came into its own with the development of larger, more efficient, high-bypass ratio turbofans like those used on the 757 and 767. "We have no infatuation with twins," commented Mike Bair, 777 chief project engineer at the time. "We could have done anything we wanted, and we would have. Based on everything we saw, the twin was right." Part of the reason was the availability of suitable engines. All three of the major engine makes—General Electric, Pratt & Whitney, and Rolls-Royce—had already declared their willingness to develop the massive new powerplants that the big twin would need. The evolutionary progress of engine power throughout the 20th century had always been upward, and they saw no reason for it to stop at the high 60,000 pounds of thrust levels of the late 1980s.

Although suitable engines were available in the trijet arrangement category, Boeing rejected the configuration on cost grounds. This was mainly due to the cost and complexity of designing the huge "banjo"-shaped fitting for the tail engine. The quad-jet configuration was dismissed because totally new 40,000 pounds of thrust class engines would have to have been developed.

Having finalized the number of engines, and been told by its working together team that a 747-like width was required, Boeing then defined the fuselage cross-section. This was finalized at 20 feet, 3 inches and was

The "Iron Bird" was one of several innovative laboratories in which the 777 systems were developed, tested, and perfected well before the first aircraft was even under construction. This view of the system reveals controls and power cables linking the tail assembly (top left) and the left wing (right). The rig was controlled by a dedicated cockpit simulator that evaluated the response of the control surfaces to the aircraft's fly-by-wire flight control system. OPPOSITE: The fourth 777 airframe began "flying" in this fatigue test rig in January 1995. Air was pumped into the structure at pressures up to 8.6 psi in less than 15 seconds, before being reduced once more to ambient pressure. The cycle was repeated day and night until more than the equivalent of two lifetimes in service had been built up.

perfectly circular, rather than the traditional Boeing contoured ellipse. The circular cross-section, the first for any Boeing airliner since the Model 307, was simpler, stronger, and less prone to fatigue. It was also easier to make because no fairings were needed to smooth out the join between the different radii of the two sections.

The wing presented unique challenges of its own. The overall size of the 767-X was, by now, much larger than anything Boeing had previously envisaged. In fact, given the direction in which its airline advisory board was pushing it, the new aircraft was quickly becoming much more than a DC-10/L-1011 replacement. With a substantial wing, new technology engines of unprecedented thrust and the wide fuselage, Boeing suddenly realized the 767-X gave it the chance to penetrate several markets with a single basic design.

The wing therefore needed to be large enough for future growth, yet still had to be small enough to meet American's DC-10 gate size restriction. It seemed an impossible combination yet Boeing managed to solve it by designing a folding wing, just like a carrier-based aircraft. The option allowed some operators to be able to fold the wing as the aircraft moved close to the gate. Normal wingspan was set at 199 feet, 11 inches, but the folding tips reduced this to 155 feet, 3 inches.

Set free to design the wing for optimum cruise conditions, the Boeing team then refined the wing for higher speed—one of the airline requirements established early on. The resulting supercritical wing was swept back at 31.6 degrees and given a pronounced amount of aft-loading. This reflected the relatively large amount of lift generated toward the trailing edge and was clearly visible in the scooped-out appearance of the underside of the wing around the flaps. The wing was designed for Mach 0.83 cruise, but proved to be faster than expected in flight tests with a capability for around Mach 0.84.

While the fuselage was being pumped up with air, the rest of the structure, including the wing, was repeatedly pulled, pummeled, and twisted. The specially programmed torture treatment simulated a complete flight from taxi, takeoff, and climb out to cruise, descent, and landing. The tremendous repeated stresses were measured by more than 1,000 strain gauges attached to various parts of the structure.

applicants were asked to make their last presentations from October 12 to 14, 1990. Airbus was there offering the A330, while McDonnell Douglas pitched the MD-11. Like the Boeing 767-X team, the other manufacturers were supported by the engine makers with a raft of powerplant options. These included General Electric's GE90 (for the 767-X) or CF6-80 family, Pratt & Whitney's PW4084, PW4164, or PW4460, or Rolls-Royce's Trent 700 and Trent 800. Altogether, United faced 33 different engine-airframe combinations, forming what the airline's 777 program manager, Gordon McKinzie, later termed a "matrix migraine."

The two winners were Boeing and Pratt & Whitney. On the afternoon of Saturday, October 14, United announced a multibillion-dollar deal with Boeing for 34 Pratt & Whitney-powered 777s plus options on a further 34. The Boeing board met on October 29 to formally launch the 777 and set the seal on a new chapter in Boeing jetliner history.

DESIGN, BUILD, TEST

To build the radical new jetliner, and to meet the ambitious goals set for the program, Boeing realized it would have to institute equally radical changes within itself. The effort spanned everything from a major expansion of the Everett facility and the building of new integrated laboratories, to the use of computer-based design on an unprecedented scale.

Almost $1.5 billion was spent on doubling the size of the Everett site to take two 777 assembly lines alongside the existing 747 and 767 lines. The construction task involved the pouring of 275,000 cubic yards of concrete, or enough to make 44 miles of four-lane highway. Enough steel (85,000 tons) was used in the expansion to build a skyscraper twice the size of the Empire State Building in New York. Further south, in Seattle itself, the company also invested $370 million in an Integrated Aircraft Systems Laboratory (IASL). The lab was packed with prototype aircraft systems, all linked together in a way that would replicate the functioning

Boeing was convinced the big twin would meet United's stringent requirements, which called for multirole performance. Its DC-10 replacement was actually needed to achieve more than the original trijet. Not only was the new aircraft needed for routes such as Chicago to Hawaii and Chicago to Europe, it was also expected to fly with a full load from Denver, Colorado, on a hot day, direct to Hawaii. The Hawaii flights were the "hidden" factor in the requirement, as they made "day one ETOPS" a prerequisite.

The acid test was a marathon, 70-hour final selection at a hotel in Chicago where all of the real thing. This was so convincing that the IASL set-up earned the nickname "aircraft zero," or "the skinless aircraft," by Boeing employees.

The IASL formed a crucial element of Boeing's new philosophy with the 777. This honored the agreement established from day one with United, which called for a "service-ready" aircraft capable of full operations from the very first day in service. It was the IASL's job to uncover every conceivable problem or bug in every system, before the first 777 even took to the air. At least, that was the plan. Within its 518,000 square feet of floor space, the lab tested 57 major systems, 3,500 line replaceable units, and 20,000 additional parts supplied by 241 companies in America and 11 overseas countries. The IASL contained 70 dedicated test stations and was backed up by 8 subsystem integration facilities. These tested major units such as landing gear, cabin management, electrical power generation, brakes, leading edge/trailing edge, electronic engine controls, autopilot/flight director, and the aircraft information management system (AIMS).

Three more "super labs" offered further chances to test big systems. These included the system-integration lab, which checked the function and interoperability of the electrical, avionics, and sensor systems, the cockpit simulator lab, and the flight controls test rig. This last lab, nicknamed "The Iron Bird," was used to validate the fly-by-wire flight control system.

The 777 was also Boeing's first 100 percent "paperless" design, thanks to the use of a computer-based design tool called CATIA. Developed jointly by IBM and Dassault of France, CATIA was used to ensure a first time fit between parts, thus eliminating expensive rework. Designs held in the database

To make it easier for assembly workers to construct the upper crown of the fuselage, Boeing developed a turn machine to tip the entire subassembly upside down.

The 777's vast wings are mated to the Section 44 center body before progressing down the assembly line to final body join. The wingspan is almost 200 feet and has an area of 4,628 square feet.

To check that the movement of a human would be unhindered in the cyberspace representation of cluttered areas like the avionics bay, the system even contained a large, computer-generated maintenance man who was variously termed "CATIA-man" or "Robocop." At peak stages in the design of the 777, more than 2,200 CATIA workstations were networked into a cluster of eight IBM 3090-600J mainframe computers—the largest cluster in the world at the time.

All the international and national suppliers to the program also hooked into the same database using the CATIA network. These included three Japanese companies: Fuji, Kawasaki, and Mitsubishi Heavy Industries, which between them accounted for 20 percent of the airframe under a joint company called the Japan Aircraft Development Corporation. The group signed a final agreement with Boeing in May 1991 covering the manufacture of most of the 777's fuselage panels and doors, wing center section, wing-to-body fairing, and wing in-spar ribs. Major international suppliers included Italy's Italy, Brazil's Embraer, Australia's Aerospace Technologies and Hawker de Havilland, Bombardier's Northern Ireland–based Shorts, and Singapore's Aerospace. Later arrivals on the scene, several years into the program, included British Aerospace, which was contracted to make the leading edges of the wing.

As befitting the first digitally designed Boeing jetliner, the aircraft itself used more digitally based systems than any of its forebears. The aircraft was controlled by a FBW flight control system, which electrically signaled slats, flaps, spoilers, control feel units, and the trimming tailplane as well as inboard flaperons, outboard ailerons, elevators, and rudder. In normal flight, the flight guidance commands to the system were generated by Rockwell Collins triple-redundant digital autopilot/flight directors. The FBW control laws and the cleverly programmed commands that kept the aircraft within a protected "envelope" (within which the airframe was never overstressed) were shaped by three primary flight control computers

were formed into three-dimensional solid images and projected together with adjoining pieces on the screen. Operators were able to detect any interferences, say between ducts and wire bundles, as the design came together and before any hardware was actually committed to production. Boeing found it hard to believe in CATIA at first and built a mock-up of the complex Section 41 nose area for verification of its new tool. The results were so good that plans for a similar Section 43 mock-up were dropped.

China Southern's first 777-200 awaits its GE90 engines as it nears the end of the final assembly line in the 40-25 building at Everett. The airline, based in Guangzhou, ordered six aircraft. BELOW: The tall triple-axle main gear required a separate design and test effort in its own right. The 777 was the first western-built production jetliner to be developed with a six-wheel, main bogie. The only other commercial jetliner to share this feature was the Tupolev Tu-154.

provided by GEC-Marconi Avionics. Each of the three computers contained three 32-bit microprocessors made by different manufacturers (Motorola, Intel, and AMD). Each microprocessor module made up a "lane," and each of the three lanes made up a "channel." Each lane was compared with the others in its channel to make sure the system was behaving. If the computers did not like what they sensed, they would "vote" with each other to override the defective unit, thereby maintaining full authority.

All commands were electrically signaled to 31 hydraulic, fully powered control surface actuators made by Teijin Seiki America. Commands to the power control units, made by Parker Bertea and Moog, were produced by three Lear Astronics and Teijin Seiki actuator electronics units. A fourth analog channel was also added, which directly signaled the units from the control columns and rudder pedals in the cockpit.

The entire FBW system was backed up with several layers of redundancy. Normal operating mode was through the autopilots, primary flight computers, and actuator control

electronics. If for some reason the inertial units and standby attitude sensors failed, the pilots could take manual control through the digital primary flight computers. A second degraded control mode, which bypassed the FBW system, operated by connecting to the direct analog link between the cockpit and the actuator control electronics. In case of a total failure, old-fashioned wires connected to the tailplane incidence mechanism and two wing spoiler panels provided some limited control in pitch and roll.

The computers were programmed to protect the aircraft from overstressing by preventing it from going too fast or too slow, or from turning too steeply. If the bank angle exceeded 35 degrees and the controls were released, the system would return the bank angle to 35 degrees. Stall protection was provided by a pitch axis control law called C★U. This held the aircraft's airspeed and responded with changes in the pitch attitude if the speed varied, rather than the alternative method adopted by Airbus, which effectively centered on holding pitch attitude.

The FBW system was linked to the rest of the aircraft's nervous system of sensors through an advanced dual triplex digital ARINC 629 databus network. This heart and brain of this system was the AIMS made by Honeywell. The AIMS was made up of two identical cabinets for redundancy. Each contained the processing equipment needed to collect, format, and distribute onboard avionics information, including the flight management system, engine thrust control, digital communications management, flight deck displays, and general systems monitoring. The displays, also made by Honeywell, were another first for Boeing. The large screens were made up from liquid crystal flat panel displays rather than the heavier cathode-ray tube (TV) displays of previous generations. Five were arranged 747-style across the flight deck on the main panel, two showing primary flight displays, two showing navigation displays, and the fifth indicating the crew alerting system display. The center console was also fitted with two FMS control and display panels as well as a multifunction display used to interface with the AIMS.

BIGGEST FANS

As the design of the 777 crystallized, it soon became obvious to the engine makers that the world's biggest twin would require the world's most powerful jet engines. The true extent of the challenge grew as Boeing's expanded family plan revealed itself. If everything came to pass, the thrust requirements would potentially go all the way from 77,000 pounds to beyond 100,000 pounds. This was unexplored territory and the engine makers knew that nothing less than a completely new generation of giant turbofans would do.

Pratt & Whitney was first off the blocks with its launch order from United, though both General Electric and Rolls-Royce were never far behind. To ensure it could reach the thrust targets, and to meet the short development timetable that called for first flight in mid-1994, Pratt & Whitney decided right from the start to pursue a derivative of its recently developed PW4000 family. The only significant differences between the newer PW4000 and its precursors was a radical increase in overall size and the adoption of wide chord, clapperless fan blades. The huge fan, measuring 112 inches in diameter, was around 18 inches larger than the next biggest member of the family powering the 747.

To keep in lockstep with the emerging Boeing giant, in 1989 Pratt & Whitney started work on the initial 777 engine, dubbed the PW4084. The engine was to be rated at 77,200 pounds for the first United aircraft, but to make sure it had instant room for growth, Pratt & Whitney planned to certify the powerplant at 84,600 pounds thrust for takeoff. Even at the reduced rating, the big Pratt & Whitney turbofan was the most powerful engine ever to be used in commercial aviation when it entered service in June 1995. Almost three years earlier, in July 1992, the engine made its first run on a test stand and a month later reached thrust levels of more than 90,000 pounds.

In November 1993 the huge engine was mounted on the prototype 747 at Seattle. Boeing leased back the elderly aircraft from Seattle's Museum of Flight for a nominal fee of $1.00 for the test period. Viewed alongside the aircraft's standard Pratt & Whitney JT9D engines, which had seemed enormous when first developed in the 1960s, the sheer size of the PW4084

became apparent for the first time. The test engine was mounted on the inboard left wing position, and all watched anxiously as the flight test program began. They did not have to wait long for the unexpected. On the third flight, a massive gout of flame, followed by a large puff of

Engineers make final adjustments to the Boeing-designed nacelle as a Pratt & Whitney PW4084 is hung on the wing of a United 777 as the aircraft nears completion in Everett. At full power, this engine could suck in around 2 million cubic feet of air per minute!

black smoke, belched from the engine just after takeoff. The PW4084 had suffered a surge, in which the pressure gradient through the engine was briefly reversed. This caused the flow to reverse and the engine to backfire.

The event provided fuel for critics of the large twinjet project, who voiced safety concerns; however, both Pratt & Whitney and Boeing rejected the criticisms saying this was exactly why test programs were needed. The problem, in this case, turned out to be a tiny gap that opened up between the compressor and the casing. Differential rates of expansion had caused the casing to expand faster than the compressor rotor. This was solved by limiting the amount of rotor cooling, thereby matching the expansion rates. Within three months, another problem cropped up when an engine on a test stand twisted in its mounts during a violent fan-blade off-test. The force of the detaching blade hitting the containment ring was roughly equal to that of a car impacting a wall at 80 miles per hour. The engine casing was stiffened to make sure that any torque would be safely contained by the

engine in the event of a similar failure and not transmitted to the attachments holding the engine to the wing.

Pratt & Whitney put 22 engines through a dedicated test program to ensure all the bugs were well and truly ironed out of the powerplant before entry-into-service. For certification, the engines racked up more than 2,500 hours and the equivalent of 6,000 takeoffs and landings. The tests included some of the most stringent ever undertaken. Flocks of dead birds and single birds weighing up to 8 pounds were fired into the engine at more than 200 miles per hour, and millions of gallons of water representing a freak storm rate of 28 inches per hour were sucked into the engine at full power. The engines were even deliberately made to run out of balance at double the normally allowed vibration levels.

The overall low-risk benefits of the Pratt & Whitney approach paid off and on May 30, 1995, the PW4084-powered 777 received FAA approval for 180 minutes ETOPS, becoming the first airliner to do so at entry-into-service. In operations, the engine went on to be highly reliable, though some issues with bearing seals and other areas cropped up in 1996 and 1997.

With the PW4084 safely launched, Pratt & Whitney began focusing attention on the next higher thrust derivatives. The first of these was the 90,000-pound thrust PW4090, which was to be offered in the 88,000- to 94,000-pound thrust range for the 632,500-pound take-off weight version of the 777-200 as well as the stretched 777-300. This increased gross weight (IGW) -200 version had originally been termed the "B market" aircraft by Boeing, while the stretch was aimed at the 747 Classic replacement market. The extra power for the PW4090 was derived from an improved high-pressure compressor and some material changes to permit higher operating temperatures.

Development on the higher thrust engine proceeded smoothly and it entered flight test on the third 777-300, WB531, in November 1997. The test effort, lasting around 200 hours, was completed early the next year and certification was granted in mid-1997. The first PW4090-powered 777-300 was delivered to All Nippon Airways shortly after.

The next growth phase, however, proved more difficult than expected. At the insistence of Korean Air, which had selected the highest weight -300 on offer, Pratt & Whitney had embarked on the development of the PW4098. This was the highest thrust version yet offered, at 98,000 pounds, and was expected to be certified on the -300 in September 1998 after about 400 hours of testing and certification. The engine was

"Open wide." A giant General Electric GE90 threatens to swallow a 737 at London Heathrow as British Airways line engineers get their first real look at the cavernous intake and 123-inch-diameter fan. Including its nacelle, the GE90 is approximately as wide as the fuselage cross-section of the Boeing single-aisle family.

based on the PW4090 core but had two additional low-pressure compressor stages, making seven in all, and improved three-dimensional aerodynamics to increase mass flow and higher thrust.

The flight-test program got underway in February 1998 on the 777-300 testbed, WB551. Evaluation of other PW4098 engines on the ground meanwhile began to show troubling results. Cracks were discovered in the ninth stage stator of the high-pressure compressor during a 150-hour endurance stress test. The discovery immediately delayed engine certification, which had been set for March 1998, and the problem was cured by using forged stators in place of less expensive cast units. More trouble followed. The engine faced a critical bird strike test in which several birds were fired into the engine at once, simulating an encounter with a flock. The birds were fired and, to Pratt & Whitney's dismay, the engine failed to maintain sufficiently high thrust for long enough to allow the crippled aircraft to fly around the pattern and return to land. "We took two birds down the core, and that's never happened to us before," said Bob Leduc, Pratt & Whitney vice president of programs.

Changes made to the stators and high-pressure compressor clearances as a result of these tests were passed with certification in July 1998. The revised engine was then cleared for flight tests on the -300 and, once more, problems cropped up. This time the engine encountered heavy rubs during simulated single-engine rejected takeoffs. The method of simulating the failure was to simply cut the fuel supply to the engine. This caused the engine to surge, with resulting rubs on the blade tips and walls of the low and high-pressure compressor sections. Pratt & Whitney felt the fuel chop simulation, which was not a specified certification requirement, had exposed a new situation which all three of the engine makers would have to deal with when it came to the huge new engines. The heavier mass and inertia of the bigger engine had caused unforeseen problems with this test, which previous lower-thrust 777 engines had passed without incident. "It is a phenomenon for the industry, not just for us," said Leduc who expected GE and Rolls-Royce to be asked to add fuel chop to their development procedures.

The revised engine, with adjustments to the turbine section and slightly reduced operating line for the high-pressure compressor, was set to restart flight tests in the second quarter of 1999. First deliveries to Korean Air were expected to begin around August or September 1999, roughly a year later than originally scheduled.

General Electric faced different problems of its own. The engine maker had taken the biggest gamble of all by announcing in January 1990 that it was launching an all-new engine for the 777, rather than attempting to squeeze more power from the CF6. With a massive, 123-inch-diameter fan, the GE90 was by far the largest aero-engine in the world. Together with the surrounding nacelle, the huge GE90 fan made the engine roughly the same width as the fuselage of the Boeing single-aisle family. The reason for such a large diameter was the large bypass ratio of more than 9:1, which GE selected for the engine. This compared to 5:1 typically found in most second-generation, huge bypass turbofans and was simply a measurement

ABOVE LEFT: Rolls-Royce grew its Trent 800 to 92,000 pounds of thrust for the 777-300, as seen here on the first Cathay Pacific test aircraft, WB502. The Trent hollow blades are made using a specially developed process called super-plastically formed, diffusion bonding. In this technique, two panels are bonded around three edges and inert gas is pumped into the gap between the panels. The blade inflates and is twisted at the same time to produce its 3-D shape. ABOVE: The GE90 was the first General Electric-built commercial jet engine to be fitted with wide chord, clapperless fan blades. As the blades were so huge, GE crafted them from lightweight carbon-based composite materials rather than the traditional titanium. Some titanium was used, however, to protect the leading edges of the nonmetallic blades from being damaged by runway debris.

Two Trent 890s power an Emirates 777-200IGW out of Dubai on a midafternoon departure to Bangkok.

of the air traveling through the fan duct divided by the airflow through the core where the jet reaction took place. The enormous fan contributed to an overall pressure ratio of more than 40:1. This was a measurement of the difference in pressure between the ambient air and the gas exiting from the engine compressor.

The fan blades were not only long, but wide. Like Pratt & Whitney, GE decided it was time to adopt a similar practice to Rolls-Royce and used wide chord blades. GE opted to use composite materials to keep the weight of such large blades under control, however, rather than go through the expense of developing technology to produce hollow titanium blades like other companies. Other advanced technology used farther back in the engine included a 10-stage high-pressure compressor derived from a joint GE/NASA project called the Energy Efficient Engine (E3). The engine also had a new type of combustor that produced only low levels of pollutants. The dual dome combustor was aimed at reducing carbon monoxide and

hydrocarbon emissions by up to 50 percent, nitrogen oxides by 35 percent, and smoke by 50 percent.

The first core engine ran in November 1992, followed by the first full-up engine run in March 1993. The following month it achieved a phenomenal thrust level of 105,400 pounds in testing and, by the end of the year, was making its first flights on GE's specially modified 747 testbed at Mojave, California. Like the Pratt & Whitney engine, the GE90 encountered rubbing. This time the problem occurred in the high-pressure turbine where cracking later cropped up due to vibration in the midseal area. The earlier rubs also led to the failure of a fourth-stage, low-pressure compressor in the 747 flight tests. Clearances were increased while planners accelerated work to certify and expand the engine to 92,000 pounds of thrust.

Certification of the baseline engine continued to prove complicated, however, mainly due to issues surrounding the clearance of the big composite blades. Nothing like this had been certified before, so GE was

the pioneer. Eventually, after repeated reruns of bird and blade-off tests, a slightly revised design with a titanium leading-edge cuff was cleared and the engine was ready to begin flight tests on the 777. These duly began on February 2, 1995, more than two months later than planned due to the certification issues. Following a long, sometimes arduous certification effort, the first GE90-powered aircraft was handed over to British Airways in November 1995.

British Airways began revenue services with its first aircraft on November 17, 1995, on the London-Dubai-Muscat service. Although the engine generally performed well, fuel burn was slightly higher than expected and GE promised further development to improve performance. Many of the upgrades were incorporated into the 92,000-pound rated GE90-92, which was delivered in early 1997 on the first of British Airways' 777-200IGW versions. At one point later that year, however, British Airways withdrew its 777s from trans-Atlantic operations because of "teething problems" with excessive wear on some gearbox bearings on the

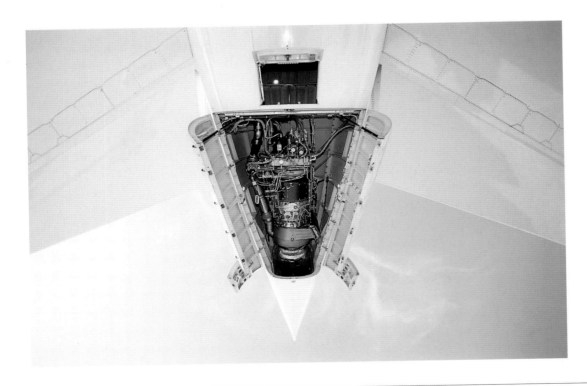

engine. Although the aircraft later returned to long-range over-water routes, a newly delivered GE90-powered Air France 777-200IGW was forced to divert to Tenerife in July 1998 en route from Brazil to France. A bearing problem was later identified as the cause of the incident.

GE embarked on an aggressive upgrade of the compressor aimed at a 2 percent fuel burn improvement and a 20-degree Fahrenheit increase in exhaust gas temperature margin. The improved compressor incorporated three-dimensional aerodynamic vanes, blades, and variable stators, derived in part from advances made on the CFM56-5BP. Clearances were also slightly altered on the low-, high-pressure turbine, and fan. The newer engine standard, which was aimed at 777-200IGW operators from

2000 onward, was expected to yield up to 10,000 hours extra life on wing. Perhaps more crucially, it offered GE a bridge to potential future growth to higher thrust levels. Up to this point, GE had been reluctant to commit to higher growth because of doubts over the size of the market. This impacted sales as potential customers were discouraged from selecting the GE90 because it had no discernible future and the move gave them reassurances that the engine program was still very much alive.

Rolls-Royce meanwhile was beginning to reap rewards with the Trent 800 on the 777. A derivative like the Pratt & Whitney engine, the Trent retained the triple-shaft philosophy to which the United Kingdom manufacturer has stuck through thick and thin. Rolls-Royce was convinced that the three-shaft principle (a low-, high-, and intermediate-pressure system) allowed the mechanics of the engine to be matched more closely to the operating efficiency of the full engine cycle. The triple-shaft design seemed to be coming into its own as the power levels rose. With the Trent 800 design, the largest version yet developed, for the first time the Rolls-Royce engine was both smaller and lighter than the competing products.

Because the three-shaft engine is often more compact than the longer two-shaft engine, it does not bow or flex in the same manner during rapid changes in thrust setting. Rolls-Royce said that this helped maintain good engine performance because the engine stayed rigid and did not rub, thereby avoiding gaps, leakage, and loss of efficiency.

Although Rolls-Royce reeled from the loss of the British Airways contract to GE, the marketplace believed the technical—if not the financial—argument, and it staged an impressive recovery by establishing a wide and varied customer base in Asia, the Middle East, and finally, North America. Crucial contracts were won from Cathay Pacific, Malaysia Airlines, Thai Airways International, Singapore Airlines, and Emirates. Most important, given the subsequent collapse of the Asian economies, Rolls-Royce also managed to secure vital long-term deals with American and Delta.

Like its competitors, the Trent 800's most distinguishing feature was its 26-blade wide-chord fan set. Unlike the other companies, which had only just stepped into the field of wide chord fan design, Rolls-Royce had been working on newer fan designs since the first wide chord blades were developed for the RB.211-535E4 engine in the 757. The result was the superplastically formed, diffusion-bonded, hollow titanium design used for the Trent 800.

The Trent 800 was designed by 1993 and made its first run later that year. In 1994, with the weight and range expectations of the 777 growing all the time, Rolls-Royce decided to raise the certification thrust level from 84,000 pounds to 90,000 pounds and accelerate development by three months.

These goals were achieved and Rolls-Royce became the first to be cleared for flight at 90,000 pounds thrust in January 1995. The company was so confident, in fact, that it hoped to gain first flight on the 777 without having to go through a flying testbed at all. Boeing had seen what the flying testbeds had unearthed on the PW4084 and GE90 programs, however, and insisted on Rolls-Royce going through the same treatment. The old 747 was therefore rolled out of retirement again and the Trent 890 flown on it for a short 20-hour test effort in early 1995.

Everything went smoothly and two Trent 890s powered a Cathay Pacific 777-200 for the first time on May 27, 1995. The flight lasted 5.5 hours during which the aircraft reached 33,000 feet and a cruising speed

The side-mounted APU exhaust was designed to reduce ground noise and prevent ingestion of snow, ice, and antifreeze fluids. It also minimized the chances of back pressure through the APU, which would have caused it to surge.

A Thai Airways International 777-200 approaches runway 13 at the old Hong Kong Kai Tak International airport. Thai was one of the first airlines to select the 777 and ordered 14. Eight of these were later converted to the stretched -300.

of Mach 0.6 (around 420 miles per hour). It also included relatively violent engine "slam" accelerations and decelerations as well as engine relights. The major disappointment came at the end of this very successful first flight. The postflight inspection at Boeing Field revealed small cracks in the aerodynamic fairing over the aft part of the strut connecting the engine to the wing. This area of structure, a Boeing responsibility, was redesigned to cure the vibration problem that had led to stress on the pylon. This delayed the Trent program by about a month.

As the Trent program gathered pace, the Cathay Pacific aircraft began its 90-cycle portion of the Rolls-Royce Trent/777

ETOPS reliability testing on January 31, 1996. All three engine/airframe combinations were run through this accelerated test phase to achieve ETOPS at entry-into-service. The Trent 800-powered 777 was certified in March 1996 with first delivery to Thai taking place later that month. The Trent 892 was granted 180 minutes ETOPS by the FAA in October 1996, the final trial involving eight 180-minute single-engine diversion flights for a total of 24 hours single-engine flying. This equated to all the diversion hours accumulated during the first five years of 767 ETOPS operations.

Emirates took delivery of the first Trent 892-powered 777-200IGW early in April

1997. A few days earlier, on March 31, a Trent 892-powered Malaysian aircraft set two world records with a flight from Seattle to Kuala Lumpur. The aircraft set the longest great-circle distance without landing at 12,455 miles and speed in an eastbound direction was set at 553 miles per hour.

The worst incident to befall a Trent-powered 777 early on in the program's life occurred early in 1998 when an engine failed dramatically on an Emirates aircraft during takeoff. An inspection revealed that the wrong type of compressor blade had been installed (for a lower power Trent 800 version) and failed as a result. The engine maker rushed to make the Trent 892 blade standard to "avoid any repeats." By late 1998, the engine was otherwise performing well with the only other unplanned removal caused by a "rogue vibration indicator." Dispatch reliability

had reached 99.96 percent and total fleet hours were expected to top 900,000 hours by the end of 1999 as the fleet numbers mushroomed. The manufacture of Trent 700 and 800 engines was meanwhile stepped up from 55 in 1998 to 90 in 1999, some of which were the new 95,000-pound thrust Trent 895. With this engine Rolls-Royce won back 777 business from British Airways, which selected the powerplant over the GE90 to power its new -200ERs.

THE 200S AND 300S

After being unveiled to 100,000 Boeing workers, families, and guests on April 9, 1994, the first 777-200 was prepared for its first flight. This eventually came on June 12 when, at 11:45 a.m. the first aircraft, WA001, took to the sky under the command of 777 chief pilot John Cashman and director of

China Southern inaugurated ETOPS flights from mainland China to the United States with its GE90-powered 777-200IGWs, one of which is pictured at the end of its long trans-Pacific journey at Los Angeles International.

flight test Ken Higgins. The 3-hour, 48-minute maiden flight was a record for an all-new Boeing jetliner and set the standard for a fast-paced test effort that was to involve nine aircraft from June 1994 to early 1996. The combined effort would cover more than 4,900 flights totaling 7,000 hours.

The early test aircraft contained 22 racks of computer consoles and instruments capable of collecting more than 50,000 different parameters. The data system itself weighed 34,000 pounds and included more than 100 miles of wiring.

The flight tests went without a hitch for much of the time, but produced some unexpected results. At one stage a temporary ceiling limit of 25,000 feet was placed on the 777 by the FAA after two incidents of cabin decompression occurred within hours of each other in Hawaii and Seattle. Both were related to the failure of a check valve in the air conditioning system and were fixed with the installation of a modified duct clamp.

Flight tests also revealed the need for some minor changes to improve handling. These involved the installation of vortex generators to reduce buffet when landing flaps were deployed. They also included the alteration of the leading-edge slat angle to cure a poststall pitch out to the left, as well as some "tweaks" to the flight control system. Further alterations to the yaw damper were also made after a "tail wag" tendency in the cruise was discovered in service. The mounts for the nose undercarriage doors were also strengthened to dampen vibration that had been encountered during cycling tests at high speed on the first flight.

By April 1995, the 777 was released for a world tour covering 45,890 miles. The 10-nation trip encompassed Korea, China, Hong Kong, Taiwan, the United Kingdom, South Africa, India, Malaysia, Singapore, and Thailand. On its return to Seattle, the 777 established a world speed record on the 7,850 mile nonstop flight from Bangkok. Another

An ANA 777-200 lifts off from Haneda. The airline placed orders for 28 aircraft and options on a further 12. Ten of the firm aircraft and five options were later converted to the -300, some of which were to be powered by the Pratt & Whitney PW4098.

world-speed record was achieved on June 11, 1995, when the first ETOPS-dedicated test 777 flew 5,142 miles from Seattle to the Paris air show in France in 9 hours, 2 minutes.

Boeing used the show to formally reveal plans for the next stage of the 777 family plan—the -300X stretch. Four airlines, All Nippon, Cathay Pacific, Korean, and Thai ordered a total of 31, some 20 of which were new orders and the balance either confirmations or conversions of earlier -200 orders. The -300 was a truly gargantuan aircraft and, at 242.3 feet in length, became the longest airliner ever made. It was 11 feet longer than the 747 and a scant 5 feet shy of the Lockheed C-5 Galaxy's overall length.

Boeing planned the 777-300 to have one main purpose—a replacement for its own early 747 Classics. By stretching the fuselage to accommodate 20 percent more passengers, it could seat up to 451 in a two-class configuration or a staggering 550 in all-economy. The large fuel capacity developed for the 777-200IGW (45,220 U.S. gallons) meant the leviathan could operate on routes up to 5,700 nautical miles. This gave it both the capacity and range to fly 747 trunk routes such as San Francisco to Tokyo or London to Los Angeles. The later timing of the -300 was also partly related to the availability of higher thrust engines, which had been pushed into development by the -200IGW program.

Cathay Pacific, one of the original gang of eight and a signatory of the -300 launch group, was a staunch champion of the stretch from the start. It helped convince Boeing that the compelling economics of the big twin versus the older 747 would soon encourage others to buy it. Boeing claimed the -300 would burn around 30 percent less fuel and have 40 percent lower maintenance costs than the Classic. It estimated that more than 170 stretch 777s could be required by the airlines through 2006 and made tentative plans to make as many as 28 per year by 2002.

OPPOSITE: The large flaps and six-wheeled main gear bogies appear prominent as this United 777-200 prepares to land. As launch customer, United also became the largest 777 operator by 1999 with 52 in service, or on order. BELOW: The first of 23 777-200IGWs is prepared for delivery to Saudi Arabian Airlines on the Everett ramp in October 1997.

Late evening sunlight casts a golden sheen over the finely crafted onyx features of this -200. Note the light passing through the GE90 engines, denoting the double-shafted powerplant's extraordinarily high 9:1 bypass ratio. OPPOSITE: Although the wings were swept at the relatively modest angle of just over 31 degrees, measured at the quarter chord point, the 777 was able to cruise comfortably at Mach 0.84 thanks to its advanced aft-loaded aerofoil design. The outboard 22 feet of each was also designed to be foldable, like a carrier aircraft, to enable it to fit into DC-10-sized gates. No operator ever selected the option, however.

The business of stretching the -200 was accomplished by inserting two plugs into the fuselage and redesigning the overwing Section 44. The forward stretch measured 17 feet, 6 inches and was achieved by adding 10 frames to Section 43, while the aft stretch involved adding nine frames, or 15 feet, 9 inches to Section 46. The fuselage could, theoretically, have been stretched even more, but Boeing stuck to the 33-feet, 3-inch extension to maintain a good lift margin and minimize handling problems at airports.

"The decision on a nine-frame stretch for the aft section was based on lift margin because that was the point where takeoff speeds and rotation margin came together. That allowed us to use the same length landing gear," said Jeff Peace, 777-300 program manager at the time. The size of the aft extension then determined the size of the forward plug because of its effect on the center of gravity. The longer aircraft could not rotate as steeply as the shorter -200, meaning the -300 needed more acceleration to create the same amount of lift for takeoff at equivalent weights. This, therefore, dictated the "lift margin."

Several new features sprouted from the 777-300 as a result of its extra length. The most obvious of these was the electrically actuated tail skid. Based on the same basic design as that used on the 767 (see chapter 6), the skid was augmented with the body contact sensor developed for the 757-300. Another feature, only just visible on close inspection, was a set of tiny lenses making up the ground maneuver camera system (GMCS). Although not required for certification, the GMCS was devised to help the crew taxi. It consisted of three cameras, one mounted in the leading edge of each horizontal stabilizer and the third beneath the forward cargo bay aft of the nose leg. The 777-300 was the first aircraft to be fitted with such a system, though Boeing originally considered developing one for the 747 as far back as 1968. Images from the GMCS were displayed on any three of the flight decks' flat panel displays, though those allocated to the system included the two inboard navigation displays and the main multifunction displays below the EICAS.

Another new feature of the –300 was the unusual overwing emergency exit slides. These were deployed aft and above the wing. As it inflated, the slide formed up to the door, while another part slid down to the ground. The combined slide therefore formed an angle and was even fitted with a guide rail and lights.

Major subassembly began in March 1997 and final body join of the first aircraft, WB501, took place at 1:30 a.m. on the morning of July 21. The aircraft rolled out on September 8 and prepared for first flight, which took place on October 16, 1997. The flawless maiden flight lasted 4 hours and 6 minutes and set the clock running on yet another fast-paced test program.

Early tests included diving the giant jetliner to speeds up to Mach 0.96, or around 0.02 Mach faster than the 777-200 had ever flown. The aerodynamics of the stretched –300 permitted it to be flown at a higher operating maximum cruise speed of Mach 0.89, compared to Mach 0.87 for the –200. To clear the buffet boundary beyond the normal cruise speed, the aircraft had to be tested right up to the edge of the transonic barrier.

By early December the test fleet was joined by WB531, the first Pratt & Whitney PW4090-powered aircraft. The two Rolls-Royce aircraft, WB501 and 502 had, by this stage, amassed more than 150 hours of flight testing, including a visit by 502 to the Dubai air show and the United Kingdom where it had been taken to show Rolls-Royce workers at East Midlands airport. Milestones passed included flutter and cruise performance tests as well as stalls.

The first airline to put the 777-300 into service was Cathay Pacific, which converted 7 of its first 11 777-200s into an order for the longer version. Here one of its first -300s is seen taxiing at the airline's new base at Chep Lap Kok airport in Hong Kong in November 1998. RIGHT: The -300 flight deck differed only marginally from the -200 in having a display for an onboard camera system. The cameras, mounted in the horizontal stabilizers and belly, helped the crew to taxi safely by showing them the position of the main and nose gears relative to the edges of taxiways and apron areas.

In all, the -300 test program was due to encompass around 1,500 hours of which 60 percent was Boeing work and the remainder certification flying for the FAA and JAA. The problems with the PW4098 mentioned above, however, prolonged the completion of the entire effort by almost one year. Of the total scheduled time, WB501 flew the largest number of hours. Around 500 hours was expected to be chalked up on aerodynamic testing, flutter clearance, control law stability, and takeoff performance. WB502 was focused on performance tests and validation of some updated navigation computers and other avionics, including a predictive windshear system and enhanced ground proximity warning system.

WB531, the first Pratt & Whitney aircraft, stuck to its program and cleared the PW4090 in relatively short order. In May 1998 the first delivery took place to Cathay Pacific, with subsequent handovers to ANA in mid-1998 and to Thai in December. By 1999, the aircraft was beginning to prove the sort of cost-effective performance levels it was capable of, and Boeing was confident of new sales as the 21st century began.

Testing of the PW4098-powered 777-300 was held up following the discovery of cracked stators. The revised design was then flight tested but suffered turbine rubs following a simulated failure. The resulting redesign setback first deliveries to Korean Air by around a year to mid-1999. It also illuminated new design and test challenges for all three engine makers as they approached the new territory beyond the 100,000-pound thrust level.

CHAPTER EIGHT

CREATING THE FUTURE

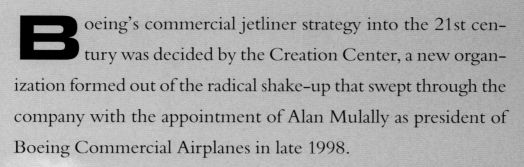

Boeing's commercial jetliner strategy into the 21st century was decided by the Creation Center, a new organization formed out of the radical shake-up that swept through the company with the appointment of Alan Mulally as president of Boeing Commercial Airplanes in late 1998.

Headed by John Roundhill, a veteran chief engineer with experience in all the company's twin-aisle projects in the 1990s, the center was set up to lead the strategy, early development, and implementation of new Boeing Commercial Airplane products

Boeing hoped the bulbous body of the C-17, originally developed by McDonnell Douglas for the U.S. Air Force, would prove attractive to the commercial world as an outsize freighter dubbed the MD-17. Built for tough missions into unprepared, dirt strips, the rugged C-17 could take C-5-sized loads into tiny runways normally useable only by C-130s. It could carry a maximum payload of more than 170,000 pounds in its military guise and was offered as a state-of-the-art alternative to aircraft such as the Ilyushin IL-76 and Antonov An-124.

One promising design for the future was the blended wing body (BWB). The concept combined wings, fuselage, and even engine nacelles to generate lift across virtually every part of the airframe. The result was a highly efficient air-lifter capable of carrying up to 800 passengers across 7,000 nautical miles, using 30 percent less fuel than an equivalent wide body.

and features. The center was also partly, or totally, responsible for product development, enabling technology, engine strategy, competitive product analysis, customer requirements, and product marketing. In short, the formation of the Creation Center marked the start of a far more holistic approach to the future aircraft strategy.

"Think of the Creation Center more as a capability than a place," said Walt Gillette, vice president of engineering, which "hosted" the Creation Center. Not only did the new unit embrace engineering, it also reported to the business development department and interfaced with all the newly created business units: single aisle, twin aisle, and customer services. It also worked closely

with the Phantom Works. This was founded originally by McDonnell Douglas as a rapid prototyping facility similar to Lockheed's famous Skunk Works. Although some of its more sensitive work remained classified, the Phantom Works enlarged and became the advanced development center for the whole of Boeing.

The setting up of the Creation Center came at a critical time for Boeing, which urgently needed strong direction by the end of 1998. Its development strategy had worked well over most of the decade, producing a string of successes, but by 1998 the future seemed less clear. This was largely due to the collapse of the Asia Pacific economies on which so much of the company's twin-aisle strategy depended. The long-haul, high-capacity demands of the Asian market were the driving forces behind the future of the 747, as well as the 777-X. The weakness of the "Asian Tigers" posed big question marks over the future of both.

The problem was compounded by competition from Airbus. The European company had launched the A340-500 and -600 derivatives, the latter seen particularly as a direct challenge to the 777-X. Boeing, on the other hand, had not been able to launch the 777-X and appeared to have dithered over the definition of the big twin. Airbus capitalized on the delay by scooping more than 100 orders by the start of 1999, even though Boeing argued that many of these were orders that would probably never have come its way, regardless of the product line-up. The same indecision also dogged the 747 growth efforts, which had virtually reached launch status as the -500X and -600X derivatives just before the Asian crisis really hit. In this case, however, the same problems also slowed the rival A3XX project.

Although Boeing remained focused on 747 derivatives, it did not neglect studies of a Large Airplane Product Development (LAPD). In mid-1997, a good two years after its last round of new large airplane studies had been dropped, it revived low-level investigations of a variety of new concepts aimed at an LAPD through a "faster, cheaper, better" initiative set up by Gillette as part of a recently formed Airplane Creation Process Strategy. This was later to be absorbed into the activities of the Creation Center, but at the time was infused with new ideas from the recently acquired engineering staff of McDonnell Douglas. The team studied McDonnell Douglas' blended wing body (BWB) as one direct result.

The BWB came to light in late 1996 during McDonnell Douglas' last full year as an independent company. The aircraft resembled a huge flying wing, but had a thick, double-deck fuselage section that was shaped to produce lift. The concept was enthusiastically embraced by NASA which, together with McDonnell Douglas, began closer studies with several U.S. universities.

The BWB offered dramatic improvements in efficiency because it integrated the engines, wings, and body into a single lifting surface. The result was an effective, high-capacity air-lifter with long-range and low operating costs.

Studies suggested a BWB could carry up to 800 passengers over 7,000 miles at a cruise speed of 560 miles per hour using only three current technology turbofan engines.

It posed several major design challenges, however, including pressurization of the noncircular passenger compartments. The design also had to be carefully tailored to reduce potentially high-drag characteristics and to enable the engines to suck in air smoothly from the boundary layer, the thin layer of air closest to the skin of the aircraft. The unusually shaped BWB also needed a sophisticated flight control system, as its stability and control behavior was actually more like a fighter than a jetliner. This could be tuned to the aircraft's advantage by allowing it to cruise with an aft center of gravity, thus reducing drag. Propulsion control systems, then in their infancy, also offered similar benefits for the BWB.

Low-speed stability and control charac-teristics were validated during test flights of

A major challenge with the BWB concept is the practical design of the interior. This is compartmentalized, rather like the spacing between the ribs of a wing or the inside of a ship, and therefore does not follow the conventional design rules adopted for circular fuselages of the current generation.

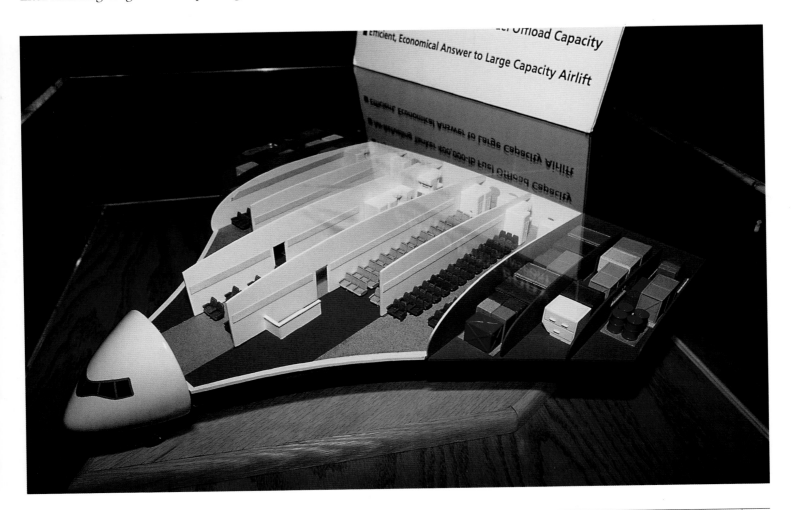

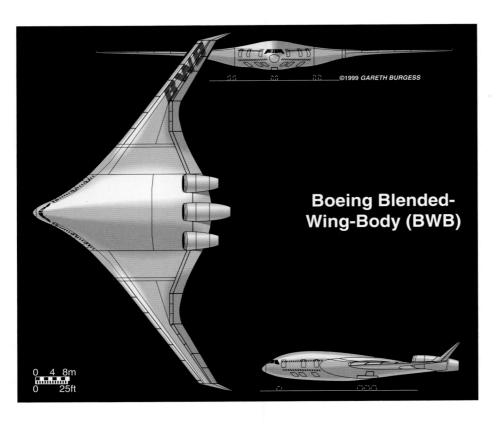

Boeing Blended-Wing-Body (BWB)

ABOVE: BWB
BELOW: 747-400, 747-400X, and 747-400Y

For the nearer term, the demands for more range and the growing threat of the A340-600 and A3XX pushed Boeing into more immediate studies of 747 derivatives. It outlined a new, ultra-long-range 8,000-plus nautical mile derivative that combined the –400 with the upper deck of the –200B. "It should be a really simple solution. We will basically take the –400F freighter and fill it with passengers and get more range. It has some unique capabilities and is relatively low risk," said the company, which dubbed it the –400ERY.

Interest was muted, however, and Boeing quickly returned to 777-X studies as the best way of meeting the ultra-long-haul demand in this seat capacity and to bigger 747 derivatives for the heavyweight solution. By December 1997, these plans were coming to fruition and the company began offering airlines a 910,000-pound takeoff-weight version dubbed the IGW (increased gross weight). Boeing hoped to make it available for delivery as early as the end of 2000 and, perhaps more important for the program's long-term future, it felt confident the –400IGW could provide the structural platform for the long-awaited stretch.

After seeing the costs of its earlier 747 growth plans spiral out of control, the company was wary about new stretch proposals. The key lesson of the –500X/600X exercise was, however, that a market did exist. The same lesson also said the market was not big enough to justify a whole new program. The company was therefore convinced that the derivative approach was the best way to ward off the threat of the A3XX, but was equally unsure about what to develop and when.

The beefed-up structure of the –400IGW, therefore, offered the chance to develop a building block approach to stretching the 747 without huge risks and costs. The first block was called the –400Y. This was a stretched fuselage version of the –400IGW incorporating 90-inch wing root plugs and a subsequently increased span. The larger wing box area automatically stretched the fuselage by around 4 feet and increased fuel capacity by a startling 100,000 pounds. Added to two fuselage stretches either side of the wing box that made the 747 31 feet longer, the result was an air-

a 17-foot span subscale demonstrator built at Stanford University. Plans for a larger "x-plane" manned NASA demonstrator, using the fuselage of an F-18 to house the pilot, were considered but later put on hold. Despite the slow down, the concept continued to attract interest for longer term air-lifter applications. The sheer efficiency of the design also meant that it remained an attractive proposition for a future subsonic jetliner from around 2020 onward.

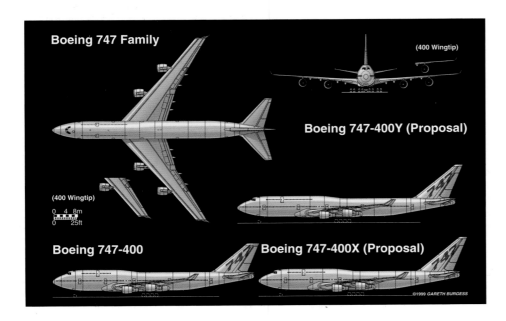

Boeing 747 Family

(400 Wingtip)

Boeing 747-400Y (Proposal)

(400 Wingtip)

Boeing 747-400

Boeing 747-400X (Proposal)

craft with a 500-passenger capacity and a range of 7,500 nautical miles.

The next step was to use the basic unstretched fuselage with the new wing, producing a much longer range aircraft. Boeing also studied a simple stretch with the modified -400IGW wing. By early 1998 the picture was still far from clear but at least it seemed to be closing in on the airline's key requirements. "Range, range, range. The thing we are consistently hearing is more range. It is starting to be a common thread through all our studies," said Joe Ozimek, leader of Boeing's product marketing group.

"We continue to believe that the market for a 500-plus-seater is between 400 and 500 aircraft. So that's not enough to support a new aircraft, but it is big enough to support a derivative. We take a 910,000-pound aircraft and do a simple stretch, which will add 70 seats. We would then let the range 'fall out' of the 7,800-nautical mile -400IGW and a have a simple stretch capable of around 6,400 nautical miles. That would solve the West Coast and north Atlantic portions of the market," he said.

This time Boeing was determined not to be sidetracked or seduced by the temptation of 777-style technology. "We are not talking about changing the systems, which is a huge driver for most of our customers. There will be some changes in the cockpit, but it will be transparent technology from the crew perspective," he added. Boeing still hoped to launch the -400IGW program officially in 1998, thus setting the ball rolling on the follow-on -400Y. This is suppose to be available by 2003, beating the A3XX into service by about a year.

By May 1998 the plan seemed to be firming up. The configuration of the -400IGW was set with a takeoff weight, not unexpectedly, of 910,000 pounds and a range of 7,700 nautical miles. Its designation was also changed to the -400X, indicating Boeing's seriousness about making this a launch candidate. It was given the -400F's strengthened outboard wing, beefed-up body frames, skin, and floor beams. The gear was also strengthened and new, larger wheels and tires were also added, marking the introduction of 777-style, 50-inch radials for the first time on the 747.

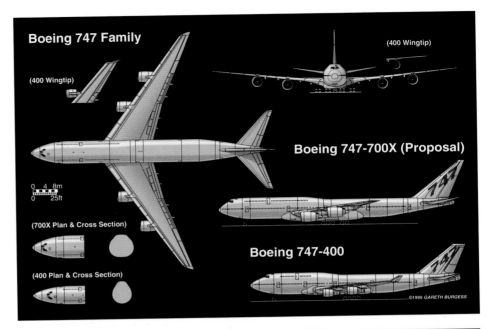

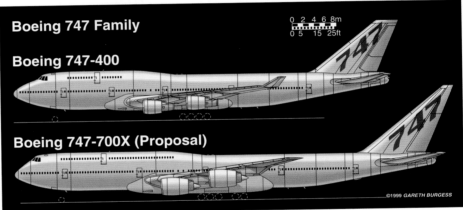

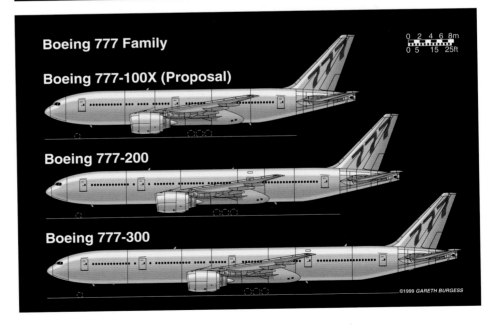

TOP: 747-700
MIDDLE: 747-400/700X
BOTTOM: 777-100X/200X/300X

To handle the weight and provide the bridge to the hoped–for stretch, the section forward of the front main wing spar and parts of Section 46 were to be strengthened. Eleven frames forward of the wing were to be strengthened, along with associated floor beams and skin panels. Much of the extra weight was made up of fuel held in two tanks, each capable of holding up to 3,180 gallons. The tanks were placed in an area normally used for potable water storage in the -400 and increased operating weight by 5,000 pounds.

By late 1998, wind tunnel tests of the stretched 500-seater were well underway, but the omens for its launch remained poor. Unfortunately for Boeing, the Asian economic crisis was in full swing, and the earliest delivery date for the -400X was pushed back from 2000 to 2001. The aircraft was still on firm offer but Ozimek said, "We are essentially waiting for someone to order it so we can launch it." The stretch, by this time, was configured with a length of around 260 feet and a span of 225 feet. Despite the Asian problem, Boeing still hoped to begin talking in detail with airlines in the first half of 1999 and, pending sufficient interest, commit to the program later that year. Target entry-into-service was late 2003, but this was heavily contingent on both the recovery of key

General Electric reversed its early decision not to expand the GE90 in 1998, and by the following year was studying a package of improvements to raise thrust to around 114,000 pounds. Some of the first steps to this new growth were incorporated into the GE90-92B, one of which is pictured on a test stand at the company's site in Peebles, Ohio, in January 1999. RIGHT: A thrusting APU was considered for the 777-200X/300X but later dropped in favor of bigger engines.

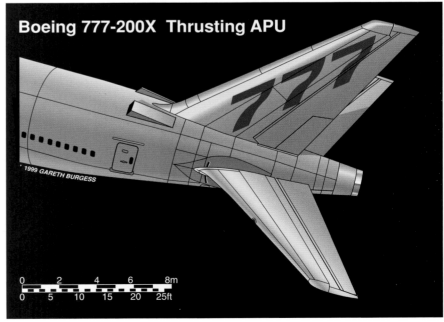

Boeing 777-200X Thrusting APU

1999 GARETH BURGESS

0 2 4 6 8m
0 5 10 15 20 25ft

Asian countries and airline satisfaction with the proposals. LAPD studies meanwhile continued quickly with the focus on 777-style, four engined airplanes.

ULTRA-LONG-HAUL 777S

While one group at Boeing wrestled with the definition and launch of the 747 derivatives, another was working hard to launch the 777-200X and -300X. From the beginning of the 777 program, the company had envisioned ultra-long-range versions capable of flying nonstop from Los Angeles to Singapore, Dallas to Tokyo, or New York to Hong Kong. The aircraft was aimed particularly at the growing trans-Pacific needs of the carriers on both sides of this vast ocean. Unlike the larger 747, however, it was to be used for new point-to-point services as well as major trunk routes between international gateways. Boeing hoped the 777X would have the same effect on the Pacific that the 767 had made on the trans-Atlantic route network in the 1980s and 1990s.

Boeing first attempted to meet the need with the 777-100X, a shortened version of the -200. The aircraft would have 10 frames (17 feet, 6 inches) removed, making it just more than 190 feet long, or slightly longer than the 767-300. The reduction in structural weight would enable the -100X to fly 250 passengers over vast distances up to 10,000 miles. Boeing initially worked toward a May 1999 in-service date, but the market began to challenge the overall wisdom of the stretch. Why not make the -200 and even the -300 capable of longer range and therefore benefit from improved seat-mile costs, they asked. Boeing knew that history was also against the concept. The only two Boeing jetliners actively shrunk both were flops, at least by Boeing's high sales standards. Only 44 747SPs, a shortened 747-200, were sold, while the 720, a shortened 707, was quickly overtaken by the arrival of the 727-200.

Development of much longer range -200s and -300s was not easy, however, and hinged on several technical and marketing breakthroughs. The key variables that dominated the debate over its final configuration were takeoff weight, range, payload, and engine power. In all cases, Boeing was going further than any manufacturer before in terms of a twinjet design.

Boeing was limited by the initial design of the 777 wing to an absolute maximum takeoff weight of around 760,000 pounds. The engine makers were not keen to pour even more money into new powerplants after suffering huge development costs on the initial 777 programs. The extra power required, varying between 15,000 and 35,000 pounds of thrust depending on the option, meant enormous investment in new fans, compressors, turbines, and materials.

General Electric's GE90 had the biggest fan of any 777 engine at 123 inches in diameter. To raise thrust even higher, GE therefore concentrated on other changes deeper within the engine. One of these was the introduction of 3-D aerodynamically shaped, high-pressure compressor blades and stators, seen here undergoing tests for the upcoming introduction of the -92B version.

Yet everyone's analysis of the market suggested it would be small. It would be even smaller if all three engine makers had to fight for shares, so all tried to negotiate for exclusivity. Paradoxically, all three knew that it would be a good marketing ploy to be on the longer range versions, dubbed the –200X and the –300X. It would extend the available power range upward through a common family of engines, giving operators confidence in the engine maker's ability to satisfy all thrust requirements across the board.

General Electric, which had shouldered the highest costs with its new GE90, showed the greatest reluctance to commit to higher growth. Rolls-Royce and Pratt & Whitney, both of which were already developing more powerful engines for the –300, pursued the –200X/300X more aggressively and signed agreements with Boeing.

Amid the gloom, the future of the derivatives suddenly appeared to brighten in March 1997 when Malaysia Airlines signed a memorandum of understanding to buy up to 15 -200Xs as part of a wider deal.

Unfortunately, no other carrier was prepared to commit to the aircraft, including Singapore Airlines, which had shown interest in converting some existing 777 orders.

Many airlines seemed concerned the 777X would not meet their ambitious performance goals. Boeing continued to define the two variants and aimed for first deliveries of the –200X in September 2000, beating the A340-500 by about a year and the –600 by 18 months. Major assembly of the –200X, with a maximum takeoff weight of 735,000 pounds, was due to begin in August 1998, with assembly of the –300X, at 715,000 pounds, starting four months later. The wingspan was extended with a new raked-tip section to 213 feet. Range with 298 passengers was expected to be more than 8,500 nautical miles for the –200X, and up to 6,800 nautical miles for the 355 passenger –300X. Some of this range was derived from extra fuel in two 2,430-gallon auxiliary tanks in the lower cargo bay. This provided a total capacity of 47,890 gallons compared to 45,220 gallons on the –200IGW.

With the potential to fly up to 20 hours nonstop ("and time to read War and Peace," said Ozimek), Boeing also began serious studies of sleeping quarters for both passengers and crew. Four main configurations were looked at, the largest of which provided sleeping space for up to 40 in specially designed underfloor "modules" in the lower lobe. It also looked at sleeping areas for crew only in the upper fuselage roof area.

In November 1997, Boeing's plans were dented when EVA of Taiwan, a significant 777X launch candidate, signed a letter of intent for the rival A340–500/600 family. With other campaigns going the same way, and definition still seemingly far off, the 777X effort began an inevitable "slide" to the right as uncertainty over performance remained. Despite urgings from Malaysia Airlines, Boeing still wanted other airlines to commit before launching, and by mid-1998 these assurances had still not come in. Entry-into-service slid from September 2000 to January 2002. "None of our customers have given us a critical entry-into-service date, and we will slow development until they do," said the manufacturer at the time.

In an effort to build more margin for weight, Boeing studied ways of improving takeoff performance. One option for the –300X was an articulating, "semi-lever" gear that held the wheels on the runway surface for longer during takeoff, effectively increasing the height of the gear. This was particularly useful for the longer –300X, which needed more runway because of the shallower angle at which it could rotate on takeoff.

Boeing also began studies of a third, tail-mounted booster engine. The extra powerplant was also considered as a potential multirole engine that could double up as the auxiliary power and thrust unit (APTU). Depending on the need, the thrust range of the study varied from 7,000 to 15,000 pounds. This mainly covered regional and business jet engines such as the Rolls-Royce Allison AE3007, the BMW-RR BR710, and GE's CF34–8. General Electric also proposed a version of its F414 fighter engine

proposed a version of its F414 fighter engine developed for the F–18E/F, but this was rejected by Boeing mainly because of its low bypass ratio.

Airlines were not very happy with the APTU plan as it threatened to dramatically increase operating and maintenance costs. They pressed Boeing to seek more main engine power instead. Boeing was reluctant to ask for higher power as both Pratt & Whitney and Rolls-Royce were actively engaged on the higher power PW4098 and Trent 8104, respectively, for the –300 and initial 777X baseline variants. Then, out of the blue in mid-1998, GE once more caught its competitors off-guard by announcing its willingness to expand the GE90 to 110,000-plus pounds of thrust.

The APTU concept and GE's move gave Boeing new options to raise the takeoff weight of the -777X to 750,000 pounds. It also threatened to leave Pratt & Whitney and Rolls-Royce behind, though Rolls felt confident the Trent 8104 still offered a good foundation for growth following its first run

Rolls-Royce perfected a revolutionary new wide chord fan blade design for its next thrust push to 104,000 pounds. The saber-shaped blades spread supersonic shock patterns farther toward the core and away from the tip, improving fan efficiency by 1 percent and reducing noise. The Trent 8104 was aimed squarely at the 777-200X/300X, which in the meantime, grew so much in proposed weight, that it was not quite powerful enough to be used. The 8104, therefore, assumed a technology demonstrator role, providing valuable research work for the both the Trent 500 project for the A340-500/600 and the follow-on Trent 8110 and 8115.

Boeing 737-700 AEW&C (Wedgetail)

0 2 4 6 8m
0 5 10 15 20 25ft

©1999 *GARETH BURGESS*

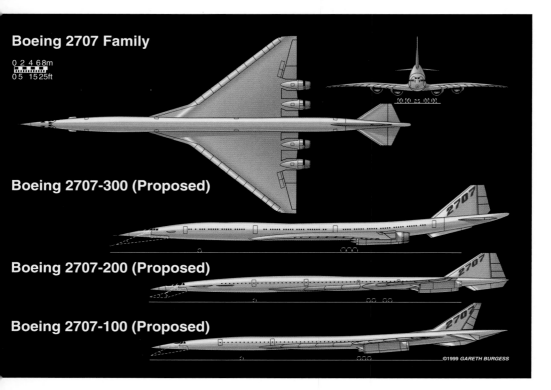

Boeing 2707 Family

0 2 4 6 8m
0 5 15 25ft

Boeing 2707-300 (Proposed)

Boeing 2707-200 (Proposed)

Boeing 2707-100 (Proposed)

©1999 *GARETH BURGESS*

TOP: 737 AEW&C Wedgetail
BOTTOM: SST

in December 1998. Fitted with advanced saber-shaped fan blades and new 3-D aero-dynamically shaped compressor stators and blades, the engine reached a 110,000-pound thrust on its second full run. As 2000 approached, the future of the 777X seemed brighter with engine makers jockeying for position. Final launch depended, as ever, on the airlines.

SINGLE-AISLE AND SUPERSONICS

The derivative approach underway for Boeing's future twin-aisle line-up was also followed with great success in the single-aisle family. The record-breaking Next Generation 737 series was due to expand by at least one major version in 2000 with the

development of the stretched -900, while studies of an extended range 757-200X and -300X family were also underway.

Another 737 variant, with even more external distinction than the BBJ, was the proposed Airborne Early Warning and Control (AEW&C) System derivative for the Royal Australian Air Force competition called Project Wedgetail. The aircraft was essentially a hybrid combination of the -700 and -800, like the BBJ, as well as the -700C combination produced as the C-40 for the U.S. Navy. Unlike the others, it also sported a large rectangular phased-array MESA radar made by Northrop Grumman.

Boeing hoped to win not only the Royal Australian Air Force competition, which involved up to seven aircraft, but also a host of other AEW competitions around the world. The first "wedgetail," as it was nick-named, was expected to be delivered as a "green" BBJ to Wichita, Kansas, in late 2000 for conversion. If selected by the Australian Air Force, Boeing planned to have the first aircraft ready for service by mid-2003.

For the longer term, Boeing's future single- and twin-aisle strategy was likely to rely to some extent on close work achieved with NASA as part of the agency's Advanced Subsonic Transport (AST) initiative. Although canceled early in 1999. this was aimed at meeting the fifth of NASA's 10 major goals for the next century—affordable air transport. It aimed to reduce the cost of air travel by 25 percent within 10 years and by 50 percent within 25 years. The multi-pronged initiative had begun in the 1990s with two major systems technology pro-grams—one aimed at reducing seat cost, the other at cutting noise. Through the former, a new set of lightweight, low-cost composite wing and airframe manufacturing methods had begun to be developed. These were the building blocks for the next phase, the Revolutionary Aircraft Efficiency Program aimed at breaking down the barriers that had prevented the design and development of radically new aircraft configurations. Both Boeing and the former McDonnell Douglas company had worked on AST concepts, the

latter having successfully developed an advanced composite wing manufacturing system shortly before its takeover.

Boeing was also closely involved in NASA's parallel High Speed Research (HSR) initiative, which was aimed at developing enabling technologies to make a 300-seat, 5,000-nautical mile range aircraft with a cruise speed of Mach 2.4. When it began in 1990, the effort envisaged a market for more than 500 HSCTs (high-speed commercial transport) by 2015, worth more than $200 billion. The focus of the effort was on lighter structures, improved high-tech systems, and low-noise, environmentally acceptable engines. This latter area had proved the stumbling block for Boeing's last supersonic transport, the 2707-200, which had reached the advanced mock-up stage when canceled in March 1971.

After completing the initial stages by mid-1998, the HSR program reached a critical watershed. It had been targeted at technologies that would have enabled an HSCT to be built and in service by 2010; however,

the targets were based on meeting Stage 3 noise levels that were progressively enforced throughout the world during the 1990s. Boeing, as a prime member of the NASA-led team, decided that meeting Stage 3 targets would not be sufficient for a 21st century jetliner. Together with NASA, it drafted new noise and performance targets which, in effect, admitted that the current and near-term engine, airframe, and materials technology were simply not up to the task. As a result, the planned entry-into-service date was shunted back at least another 10 years to around 2020. The delay threatened to postpone, or even terminate, funding for the entire venture as 2000 approached. The situation was particularly critical at the time as NASA was also looking for extra cash to prop up the International Space Station project.

Not unexpectedly, Boeing cut its SST study workforce from 250 to 50 in January 1999. Within a few days an international supersonic study team, of which Boeing was a member, was disbanded. The group

Boeing joined with other U.S. and European aerospace companies in a NASA-led effort to use a Tupolev Tu-144 to help develop precise analytical tools for future supersonic development. Test flights continued through 1998, but the program was suddenly terminated the following year when NASA's High Speed Research effort was axed to divert resources to the International Space Station. Sergey Sergeyev

Signature

Boeing's Business Jet, the BBJ, sprouted 8-foot-tall blended winglets in time for the 1998 National Business Aircraft Association show in Las Vegas. Designed by Aviation Partners, the winglets were later made standard as they produced a 5 percent fuel saving, or up to 300 nautical miles more range. The BBJ formed Boeing's entree to the corporate world, and its subsequent interest in a possible supersonic bizjet for the 21st century.

included Aerospatiale, British Aerospace, DaimlerChrysler Aerospace of Germany, Alenia of Italy, the Japanese Aircraft industry, as well as Tupolev. By February 1999, the HSR effort was finally effectively dead.

While hopes for an HSCT receded, the prospects for a supersonic business jet (SSBJ) unexpectedly emerged in 1998. Boeing's new interest in business aircraft, sparked by the BBJ, convinced it that there were more potential opportunities to explore. With BBJs selling well, Boeing also held

exploratory talks that year with Sukhoi, the famous Russian fighter design company, about collaboration on an SSBJ project. BBJ president, Borge Boeskov, said the preliminary talks were in the very early stages and that anything concrete was "a long way off." The move nonetheless proved that Boeing's supersonic ambitions were not restricted solely to dreams of HSCTs. The SSBJ studies were aimed at something a lot smaller than the HSCT. Aircraft being considered seated around a dozen passengers, had trans-Atlantic

range capability, and a top speed of approximately Mach 1.8. These goals made the SSBJ achievable in the relative near term, and this meant the prospects for supersonic civil aircraft were a lot closer within the business community than with the airlines.

CARGOES, CONVERSIONS, AND TECHNOLOGY

As the air cargo market began to show definite signs of growth in the last decade of the 20th century, Boeing widened its freighter product line to attract more business. A large part of this was due to the timely takeover of McDonnell Douglas, which had three significant cargo programs either in planning, development, or production. The first of these was the MD-11, which had achieved great popularity as a freighter. Although the production line shut down in 2000, Boeing continued to meet the demand for passenger-to-freighter conversions. Another big conversion program inherited by Boeing was the MD-10 program. Under this effort, FedEx signed a deal in 1996 with

Douglas Aircraft to convert a minimum of 60 DC-10s to MD-10s. These ex-airline aircraft, mostly from American and United, were converted in the traditional manner from passenger to freighter aircraft. The big difference, however, was in the flight deck where new processors and flat panel displays gave it a thoroughly 21st century appearance. FedEx eventually planned to have up to 120 MD-10s in its fleet by the mid-2000s, including its DC-10 fleet.

The third cargo element inherited from Douglas was the MD-17 program, a specialized freighter derivative of the U.S. Air Force's C-17 Globemaster III. The big problem with this effort was the price of the basic aircraft. The C-17 was expensive to develop, the first few aircraft costing an astonishing $300 million-plus per copy. McDonnell Douglas, followed by Boeing, had worked relentlessly to cut this cost down, and by 1999, believed it could sell the commercial MD-17 variant for around $175 million. This was still a huge amount, even compared to Boeing's own 747-400F, the world's largest general cargo aircraft in production, but the company believed it was on the verge of a significant niche market. The niche, in this case, was the growing "outsize" transport market that had been sparked into life by a handful of massive Antonov An-124 freighters. These big Russian aircraft criss-crossed the globe hauling everything from generators and cranes, to complete fuselage sections and GE90 engines.

Boeing believed a reliable, more capable MD-17 was the perfect aircraft to step in and take advantage of the growing need. As with so many other Boeing projects, the launch of the MD-17 depended on orders.

The C-17, like many military transports, was equipped with a head-up display (HUD). This allowed pilots to follow precise flight guidance cues, which were projected on the glass of the HUD, without having to take their eyes away from the windshield. By the late 1990s, these devices were starting to become more widespread on other jetliners, particularly the Next Generation 737. Led by pioneering efforts from Oregon-based Flight Dynamics with its Head-Up Guidance (HGS) system, the fleet of HUD-equipped 737s began to grow dramatically in 1998 and 1999 as airlines like Alaska, Delta, and Southwest took delivery. In 1989, American Airlines added credibility to the concept by selecting an alternative system made by Marconi for its new 737 fleet. Most of the airlines eventually expected to transfer the technology into other types within their fleets.

Other key developments in engine technology also offered the potential for great change in the future. Pratt & Whitney led the charge with a concept termed "the geared fan." As the term suggested, the engine's core was connected to the fan through a sturdy gear system. Pratt & Whitney had tried the idea out on a larger scale version in the late 1980s and

early 1990s, but dropped it for cost and maturity reasons. With improved technology available, and in desperate need of an answer to the overwhelming dominance of the CFM56, the company hit on the notion of reviving the concept for a midthrust family of engines led by the PW8000.

The PW8000's future depended on the launch of another engine, the PW6000, which was to form the core for both powerplants. The PW6000 was itself based on a military core developed as part of Pratt & Whitney's heavy involvement in the U.S. government's Integrated High Performance Turbine Engine Technology (IHPTET) initiative. The PW6000, in turn, needed an aircraft on which to be launched, and its chance came in 1998 when Airbus studied a new 100-seater to compete with the 717. After a rigorous engine selection, Airbus chose the PW6000 to power the new aircraft, which was called the A318. The program had emerged from the ashes of the AE31X, a joint program studied in conjunction with several Asian countries but which never got off the ground.

Although ostensibly launched thanks to an Airbus product, the PW6000 was expected to lead to the PW8000 early in the 21st century. This would provide Boeing with a new option in its search for low-cost, high-efficiency products from 2010 and beyond. It was also expected to stimulate the two main competitors, both of which were moving progressively toward higher bypass ratios and

While Pratt & Whitney was busy with the fan drive gear, CFM International was working on a new package of improvements to ensure future life for the popular CFM56 engine into the 21st century. The TECH56 initiative included the use of advanced 3-D compressor technology, some of which is seen in the early stages of evaluation at General Electric's Evendale site in Ohio in early 1999.

reduced stages. Pratt & Whitney planned to use the geared fan concept as the basis for a family of new-generation engines to power all future subsonic commercial jetliners.

Together with some of the technology salvaged from the NASA AST and HSR programs, the engine initiatives meant that Boeing was well placed to meet the challenge of Airbus as it marched into the next century. With almost 90 years of consistent progress and growth behind it, Boeing seemed determined to maintain its never-ending pursuit of excellence.

Pratt & Whitney's future engine strategy hinges on the development of the PW8000, an advanced geared turbofan aimed at better performance but with lower fuel burn and lower noise. Similar projects were also emerging at the other engine companies, which were beginning to look at Boeing's power requirements for the 21st century. Advanced propulsion systems will be needed for Boeing's next generation of subsonic transport designs, particularly the long-term successor or successors for the 737 and 757 families.

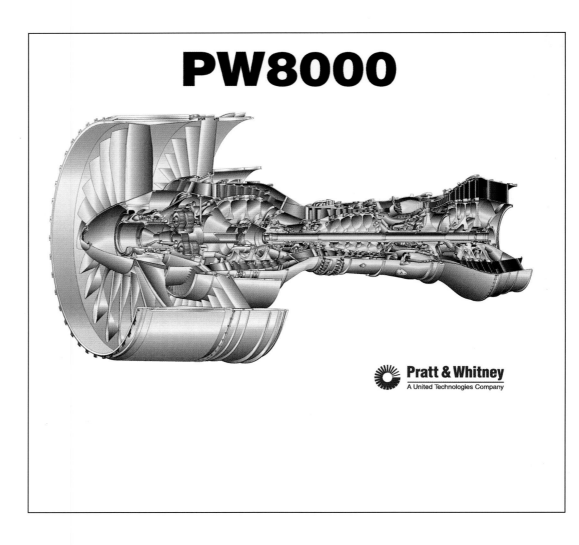

PW8000

Pratt & Whitney
A United Technologies Company

The heart of the PW8000 was a robust fan drive gear system that transferred the energy of the low-pressure spool at 9,000 rpm to the fan at the much more efficient speed of 3,200 rpm. Pratt & Whitney hoped the gear would provide it with a technical trump card that could be used to develop an entire family of new turbofans covering the 20,000- to 100,000-pound-plus thrust range.

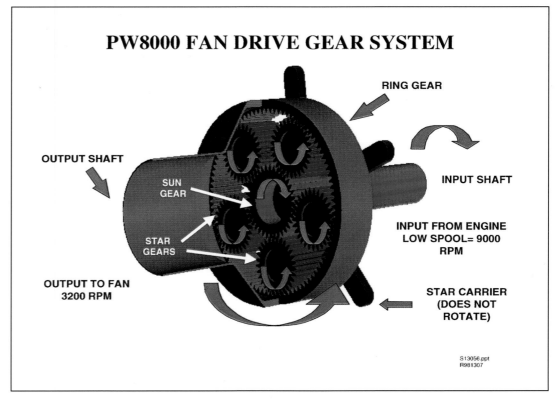

PW8000 FAN DRIVE GEAR SYSTEM

RING GEAR

OUTPUT SHAFT

SUN GEAR

STAR GEARS

INPUT SHAFT

INPUT FROM ENGINE LOW SPOOL= 9000 RPM

OUTPUT TO FAN 3200 RPM

STAR CARRIER (DOES NOT ROTATE)

S13056.ppt
R981307

INDEX

331-400, 123
Advanced Subsonic Transport (AST), 168
AE3007, 167
Aeritalia, 21
Air Canada, 87
Air France, 87, 144
Air Namibia, 20
Air New Zealand, 116
Airborne Early Warning and Control
    (AEW&C), 168
Airborne Express, 23
Airborne Warning and Control Systems
    (AWACS), 96
Airbus, 21, 25, 40, 44, 45, 74, 82,
    88–90, 92, 97, 116–118, , 125, 126,
    160, 173
AirTran, 28, 29, 36, 37
Alaska Airlines, 59, 70, 172, 173
All Nippon Airways (ANA), 12, 23, 85,
    127, 128, 136, 140, 149, 151, 154,
    157
America West, 45
American Airlines, 15, 21, 22, 70, 118,
    127, 128, 145, 172
APS2100 APU, 30
APU, 52, 77, 123, 128, 143
Arkia Israeli Airlines, 105
Asiana, 84
Atlas Airways, 92
B8F1, 122
Bair, Mike, 129
Blended wing body (BWB), 160–162
BMW, 27, 34, 167
Boeing Business Jet (BBJ), 63, 70, 71
Boeskov, Borge, 170
BR710, 167
BR715, 27, 29, 30, 33–35,
Braathens SAFE, 14
British Aircraft Corporation (BAC), 13
British Airways, 20, 76, 88, 91, 92,
    123, 127, 128, 143, 145, 148
British Midland, 59
Canadian International, 84
Carriker, Mike, 69
Cashman, John 148, 154
Cathay Pacific, 86, 92, 127, 128, 141,
    145, 151, 152, 156, 157
Caton, Doug, 48–50
CF-80C2B7F1, 122
CF34-8, 167
CF6, 83, 141
CF6-80, 132
CF6-80A, 21
CF6-80C2, 122
CF6-80C2B1F, 77
CFM International, 45, 46
CFM50, 95
CFM56 turbofan, 12
CFM56, 14, 17, 44, 45, 66, 173, 175
CFM56-3, 55
CFM56-3SX1, 46
CFM56-5, 55
CFM56-5BP, 144
CFM56-78, 46
CFM56-7B, 54, 69
China Airlines, 67, 89
China National Aero-Technology Import
    Export (CATIC), 26

China Southern, 135, 148
Classic, 51–55, 58, 59, 62, 71, 73, 76,
    151
Computer-Aided Three-Dimensional
    Interactive Applications (CATIA), 16,
    19, 34, 46, 72
Condit, Philip, 128
Condor Flugdienst, 96
Condor, 113
Continental, 120
Craig, Ray, 69
Creation Center, 160
Croslin, Tom, 31, 33
Dassult, 133
Defense Evaluation and Research
    Agency (DERA), 118
Delaney, Michael, 36
Delta Air Lines, 20–22, 70, 111, 116,
    117, 120, 123, 127, 145, 172, 173
Douglas Aircraft Company, 27
Eastern Airlines, 12, 20, 21
Emirates, 142, 143, 145, 148
Energy Efficient Engine (E3), 142
Ethiopian Airlines, 15
Euralair, 14
European airworthiness authorities
    (JAA), 36, 37, 52, 66, 69, 85, 86,
    112, 113, 157
EVA Air, 92, 167
Extended range twin operations
    (ETOPS), 44, 45, 48, 51, 52, 73–75,
    129, 132, 139, 147, 148, 151
Fanning, Art, 107, 109, 111
Federal Aviation Administration (FAA),
    36, 37, 67, 84, 86, 112, 113, 139,
    147, 149, 157
FedEx, 15, 172
Feren, John, 38
Fly-by-wire (FBW), 14, 44, 134–136
Future Air Navigation System (FANS),
    79, 102
GE90, 132, 140, 141, 143–145, 148,
    152, 164–167, 172
GE90-92, 143
GE90-92B, 164
General Electric (GE), 15, 17, 22, 46,
    63, 77, 83, 84, 122, 123, 129, 132,
    137, 140–145, 164–167, 175
Gibbons, Will, 36
Gillette, Walt, 160
Gitner, Gerald, 41
GTCP332, 123
Gucker, Jack, 47, 104
Hapag Lloyd, 63
Head-Up-Guidance (HGS), 64, 173
Hewett, Mike, 57, 65
Higgins, Ken, 57, 149
High-speed commercial transport
    (HSCT), 169
Honeywell, 80
IBM, 133
Jackson, Duane, 90
Japan Air Lines, 22, 127
Jet Airways, 55
Johnson, Lee, 34
Joint Strike Fighter (JSF), 118, 119
JT3A, 11
JT3D, 11

JT3D-7 turbofan, 13
JT8D, 12, 27
JT8D-218, 27
JT8D-7/9, 33
JT9D, 15, 21, 77, 137
KC-135R, 12
Kirchner, Dietmar, 102, 105
KLM, 28, 70, 77, 85–87
Korean Air, 84, 90, 140, 141, 151, 157
Large Airplane Product Development
    (LAPD), 160, 165
Ledue, Bob, 141
Lockheed, 126, 160
Luczak, Ralph, 36
Lufthansa, 14, 16, 86, 91
Maersk, 14, 69
Malaysia Airlines, 91, 145, 166, 167
McDonnell Douglas, 6, 18, 25–27, 65,
    74, 88, 89, 92, 118, 125, 126, 132,
    159, 160, 161, 171, 172
McKinzie, Gordon, 132
McRoberts, Jim, 65
MD-80, 27
MD-95, 39
MEA, 15
Melody, Tom, 36
Micale, Antonio, 104
Mooney, Dan, 98, 100, 101, 108, 109
National Aeronautics and Space
    Administration (NASA), 74, 161, 168,
    175
New Large Airplane (NLA), 29, 30, 44,
    54, 90
Next Generation, 47, 51, 53, 54,
    56–59, 62, 66, 67, 69, 70, 71, 102
Nicoletti, Bruce, 97
Nightingale, Patrick, 34
Norman, Greg, 71
Northrop Grumman, 47, 80, 168
Northwest Airlines, 26, 45, 73, 77, 85
Ozimek, Joe, 163
Pan American, 12, 15, 16, 18
Peace, Jeff, 152
Phantom Works, 160
Phillips, Jim, 35
Piedmont Airlines, 14
Pratt & Whitney, 11–13, 15, 20, 26, 45,
    77, 83, 122, 123, 129, 132,
    136–142, 144, 149, 154, 157, 166,
    173–175
PW2000, 20, 99
PW4000, 122, 137
PW4056, 77, 85
PW4062, 123
PW4084, 132, 136–140, 145
PW4090, 140 141, 154, 157
PW4098, 140, 141, 149, 157, 166,
    167
PW4164, 132
PW4256, 77
PW4460, 132
PW6000, 41, 173
PW8000, 173
PW901A, 77
Qantas, 13, 79, 92, 127
Queen, Hank, 119, 120
RB.211, 83
RB.211-524G/H, 22, 77

RB.211-524H, 123
RB.211-524HT, 76
RB.211-535, 111
RB.211-535E4, 145
RB.211-535E48, 98
RB.211-553C, 20
Robert, Leon, 100, 106
Rolls-Royce, 11, 17, 20, 77, 83, 84, 86,
    98, 111, 123, 129, 132, 137, 141,
    142, 144, 145, 148, 154, 166, 167
Roundhill, John, 159
Royal Australian Air Force, 168
Rumsey, Peter, 53, 54
Santoni, Frank, 154
SAS, 28, 54, 70
Saudi Arabian Airlines, 57, 88, 151
Selge, Rolf, 40
SIA, 85, 88, 91, 92
Singapore Airlines, 91, 145, 166
Skunk Works, 54, 160
Southwest Airlines, 14, 16, 28, 101,
    172, 173
Steele, Duncan, 34
Supersonic business jet (SSBJ), 170
Supersonic transports (SSTs), 16
Sutter, Joe, 74, 118
Swissair, 34, 118
Tay 650, 14
Tay 670, 27
Thai Airways International, 86, 91, 145,
    146, 151
Thornton, Dean, 84, 85
Trans World Airways, 40, 41
Transaero, 62
Transavia, 56
Trent 600, 123
Trent 700, 76, 132, 148
Trent 800, 132, 141, 144, 145, 147,
    148, 154
Trent 8104, 167
Trent 8110, 167
Trent 890, 142, 145
Trent 892, 147, 148
Trent 895, 148
Trippe, Juan, 18
Turkish Airlines, 64
U.S. Air Force, 10–12, 14, 29, 159, 172
U.S. Navy, 64, 65, 168
Ultra-high-capacity aircraft (UHCA), 89,
    90
United Airlines, 12, 18, 21, 22, 45, 88,
    91, 92, 126, 127, 128, 133, 136,
    137, 151, 172
United Parcel Service (UPS), 14, 22,
    23
USAir, 14
UTA, 19
V2500, 29, 45, 46
ValuJet, 28
Very large commercial transport (VLCT),
    89, 90
Virgin Express, 17
Welch, Jack, 63
Whitcomb, Richard T., 74
Whites, Jerry, 106
Woodard, Ron, 41, 59, 105
World War II, 9
Wyatt, Randy, 34

Models

2707-200, 169
367-80, 9
-400ER, 120
700-400Y, 162, 163
700QC, 63
707, 9, 11–13, 15, 21, 46, 57, 76
707-020, 29
707-138, 13
707-300, 11
707-324C, 13
707-400, 11
717, 6, 12, 24–30, 32–41,
717-100A, 29
717-200, 26, 29, 36, 37, 40, 41
720, 12, 15, 29
720-060B, 15
727, 12–15, 22, 44
727-100, 12, 14
727-200, 12, 14, 18, 19, 57
727-300, 19
737 AEW&C Wedgetail, 168
737 Classic, 46, 71
737, 6, 12, 14, 16, 17, 33, 43, 45, 47,
    51–53, 56, 59, 62, 64, 71, 104,
    133, 120, 129, 140, 168, 172, 174
737-100, 14
737-200 Advanced, 14
737-200, 14–16
737-230, 16
737-300, 14, 16, 17, 44, 66, 95, 105
737-300X, 46, 47
737-400, 14, 44
737-500, 14, 16, 44
737-600, 25, 66, 67, 69, 70
737-700, 45, 47, 49, 52, 57, 62, 63,
    65–67, 69, 71, 107
737-700C, 70
737-700QC, 64, 65, 71
737-800, 53, 55, 58, 62, 63–67, 70
737-900, 6, 62, 67, 70, 71
737-900X, 59
737-X, 47
747 Classic, 151
747, 14, 15, 18, 19, 56, 71, 74, 76, 77,
    80, 84, 85, 88, 91, 95, 121, 125,
    132, 136, 142, 151, 160, 163, 165
747-100, 17, 18
747-100SR, 17
747-200, 17, 19, 165
747-200B, 17, 92
747-200F, 87
747-300, 19, 74
747-400 Combi, 87
747-400, 54, 57, 73, 75, 78, 82–85, 88,
    90, 93, 101, 116, 120, 122, 162, 164

747-400D, 87
747-400ERY, 162
747-400F, 86, 87, 92, 162, 172
747-400IGW, 162, 163
747-400M, 87
747-400X, 163, 164
747-500X, 90– 92, 117, 123
747-600X, 90–92, 117, 123
747SP, 17, 20, 105, 165
747X, 162
747-X, 91
757, 18, 20– 23, 44, 48, 51, 52, 54,
    56, 59, 74, 76, 77, 80, 95, 104, 117,
    120, 129, 145, 174
757-200, 23, 95, 96, 97, 99, 108
757-200X, 168
757-300, 6, 51, 95– 98, 100, 104,
    106, 107, 109, 110, 113, 117, 119,
    152
757-300X, 168
767, 18, 20–23, 48, 54, 56, 71, 74,
    76, 80, 92, 116, 117, 119, 120–122,
    129, 132, 147, 152, 165
767-100, 21
767-200, 21, 23, 96, 98, 119, 120
767-200ER, 21
767-300, 22, 99, 110, 116, 117, 119,
    120, 123, 127, 165
767-300ER, 22, 117
767-300ERX, 116
767-300ERY, 116
767-300F, 22, 119
767-400, 117, 119, 122, 123
767-400ER, 6, 115–118, 121–123
767MR/LR, 21
767-X, 126–128, 130
777 APTU, 164
777, 21, 45, 46, 48–51, 54, 56, 57, 71,
    76, 80, 91–93, 97, 99, 107, 116,
    117, 120–123, 125, 126, 128–130,
    132–134, 136, 143, 146–149, 151,
    152, 165
777-100X, 116, 165
777-200, 88, 107, 135, 139, 140,
    145, 146, 148, 149, 151, 152, 154,
    156, 165
777-2001GW, 142–144, 147, 148,
    151, 166
777-200X, 165–167
777-300, 140, 141, 151, 152, 154,
    156, 157, 165, 166
777-300X, 151, 165–167
777-X, 160
777X, 165–168
7J7, 14
7N7-100, 20

7N7-200, 20
7X7, 21
A300, 74, 119
A300B, 21
A310, 74, 119
A310-300, 98
A318, 26, 38, 40, 41, 173
A319, 28
A320, 40, 44–46, 117
A321, 59
A321-200, 97
A329, 117
A330, 74, 116, 126, 128, 142
A330-200, 117
A330M10, 117
A340, 74, 126
A340-500, 160, 166, 167
A-340-600, 160
A340-600, 162, 167
A340-8000, 117
A3XX, 89, 90, 123, 160, 162
AE31X, 25, 29, 173
An-124, 159, 172
B-2A, 47
B-47, 9–11
B-52, 11
BR700, 27
BR710, 27
BR715, 27
C-135, 11
C-17, 159, 172
C-40, 168
C-5 Galaxy, 151
C-5, 159
C-5A Galaxy, 17
C-9B, 64
Classic 737, 58
Classic 747, 78, 118, 140
CX-HLS, 15, 16
Dash 80, 11, 12, 14
DC-10, 18, 21, 22, 122, 126–128,
    130, 132, 152, 172
DC-10-30, 117, 119
DC-6, 44
DC-7, 44
DC-8, 11, 13, 16, 26, 27, 29, 30–34,
    36, 38, 41, 44, 110
DC-9-30, 26, 27, 34
DC-9-34, 34
DC-9-90, 26, 27
DC-9X, 27
deHavilland DH-106 Comet, 11
E-6, 57
E-8, 57
F-18E, 167
F-18F, 167

IL-76, 159
KC-135, 11, 12
KC-97, 10
L-1011 TriStar 500, 119
L-1011 TriStar, 18, 126
L-1011, 122, 130
LCD, 120
Lockheed TriStars, 117
MD-10, 171, 172
MD-11, 33, 67, 74, 88, 118, 126, 128,
    132, 171
MD-12, 89
MD-17, 159, 172
MD-80, 26, 29, 45, 67
MD-81, 26
MD-87, 26, 27, 33
MD-87-105, 26
MD-90, 27, 29, 34, 45, 57, 59, 63, 65,
    67, 88, 101
MD-95, 25–29
MD-95-20, 29
MD-95-50, 29
MD-XX, 118, 119
Model 307, 130
Model 367 Stratoliner, 11
Model 367-80, 10
Model 450, 10
New Large Airplane (NLA), 88, 89
Next Generation 737, 6, 26, 43–45, 48,
    54, 62, 67, 71, 83, 85, 97, 101, 102,
    107, 117, 168, 172, 173
Next Generation 737-600, 28
Next Generation 737-700, 16
Next Generation 757, 117
NU701, 106
NU721, 108, 109, 111, 113
NU722, 112, 113
One Eleven, 13
P-1, 37, 41
T-1, 27, 31–34, 37, 39
T-2, 34, 35, 37, 38, 40
T-3, 37, 40
Trijet, 12, 14, 21, 129
Trijets, 126
Tu-144, 169
Tupolev Tu-154, 135
Twinjet, 12, 21, 26
Twinjets, 23
WB501, 154, 157
WB502, 154, 157
WB531, 154, 157
XB-47, 10